The Wave Effect

by

Janie Hopwood

*To Peggy
Thank you for every word of encouragement - each word is important!
Love you,
Janie Hopwood*

Aakenbaaken & Kent

Aakenbaaken & Kent

The Wave Effect

Copyright 2018, all rights reserved.

No part of this book may be used or reproduced in any manner whatsoever without written permission except in the case of brief quotations for use in articles and reviews.

Aakenbaakeneditor@gmail.com

This book is a work of fiction. Names, characters, places and incidents are either the product of the author's imagination or are used fictitiously. Any resemblance of the fictional characters to actual persons living or dead is entirely coincidental.

ISBN: 978-1-938436-43-7

Dedication

To Deanne Veal
the force and support behind each and every project
Thank you

Chapter 1

The elephants know. It is too calm, too sunny, too silent. In fact, the only animals around are chained up, locked up, or human. The humans might have guessed except they are too busy, too satiated, or too far from home. No one notices the lack of trumpeting, barking, hissing, chirping. The absense of everyday sounds should have been a foreboding. So, when at precisely 1:34 PM the greatest tsunami in history hits the exclusive Indonesian resort, the humans are surprised.

The wave is enormous, throwing anything not secured in solid ground into anything that is. What have been pleasure boats in the harbor become missiles slamming into buildings, slicing vehicles and piercing humans too exposed or too slow to move. Decades old hotels designed for placating the wealthiest of clientele crumble into the sea like drip castles. Chaos reigns, death grabs the day, desperation laps at the teeming masses headed no one knows where. Away, simply away.

A half a world away in New York, Rodger Madden doesn't care. He is involved in his work and safe. When the news of the disaster finally filters into his awareness, he stops briefly to send out an "oh those poor creatures" thought before dropping back into the paperwork on the upcoming merger. Rodger is the COO of Benson Enterprises, a major international company dealing in energy commodities and technologies. The company currently claims assets in fifteen different countries, and he hopes to expand that by three. He has lived and breathed this potential merger for the last three months, sometimes spending twelve to fifteen hours per day at the office. This day he is six hours in when James Stanton, the dapper head of the legal department, opens the door as he is knocking.

"Heard the news of the tsunami?"

"Yeah, bad scene. What can I do for you?" Rodger is not used to being interrupted. His glance toward James is short as his eyes rove down toward his desk and the pen in his hand taps away the seconds.

"You are aware of where this thing is, right?"

Rodger sighs. "Indonesia somewhere. So?"

"So where do you think Carl is vacationing? That uber fancy resort where he, Maria, and the kid stay is dead center of the affected area."

He now has Rodger's undivided attention. Although it is a rarity in the modern world, Carl and Maria Benson solely own Benson Enterprises. Everything – money, policy, expansion, goes through this family. Rodger runs the day to day operations, reports on possible new ventures, and oversees research and development opportunities. His standing in the company, his very job, depends on this family.

"What? Has anyone heard from them? Where is our closest office?"

Questions spew out of his mouth as possibilities blink through his brain like the flickering of a silent movie reel. *Focus man, focus*, he silently berates himself.

"No information as yet, I think we should send the head of security in the Damascus office to check it out," James replies. "He worked with Carl in Jakarta and is familiar with the area and the Bensons."

The two men look at each other. Rodger nods as if agreeing with whatever it is James leaves unsaid. "Get… what's his name on the phone immediately. I guess it is too much to hope for any communication with the resort?"

"His name is Amur Saluar and no, don't think we are likely to hear from the resort if it is even still there. I will continue to call cell numbers on a regular basis on the off chance someone answers." James withdraws silently, leaving Rodger staring at the computer and mulling future options.

It is afternoon in Indonesia before Amur is contacted and starts on route to Benkulu. It is mid-morning in New York before they receive his report. James, Rodger and two other top company officials are together discussing options when the call comes through.

"Amur," begins Rodger, "Have you found the Bensons?"

"You have no concept of what it is like over here. I am trying to get to the coast, but there are no accessible roads, no vehicles for hire, and no way to track independent people. Everything on the road is a government vehicle or one from an international care agency. I will continue to try; however, there is no way I can predict a timeline."

James looks at the frown on Rodger's face. "Do the best you can, and Amur, report in at least twice a day."

"Everywhere I have a signal, over and out." The line goes dead.

The four men in the calm, safe, New York office feel anything but calm. Each of them struggles to comprehend what the situation is now and where they need for it to go. Without speaking, the three leave the office and the COO.

Rodger presses his long finger tips together, pondering the problem. Everything about him is long, except his patience. Amur is a capable employee, of course, but his urgency to establish quick and certain contact with the Bensons, as well as getting them to a secure facility is no where near this level. Rodger has never been one to sit and wait when his life's work hangs in the balance. As if the idea pushed its way from his fingers through to his active brain, he picks up his phone, asks his secretary to order his private plane to be ready asap to fly him to the closest airport to Benkulu. He will check things out himself.

That afternoon, he boards the company jet. Phil Godwin, the company pilot, is frowning as he and co pilot Dave Campbell pour over the logistics available to them. "The closest airport that might be open is The Sultan Muhmud Badarunddla II in Palembang. Problem is we can't get through to them. I don't know if it is down, or if the communications are overloaded and they are screening calls. There is no way to tell. I can get you to Darwin in Australia, and we can try again from there, that is the best I can do. So do we go or do we wait?"

Rodger fidgets, looks at his watch, grimaces, shakes his head and says, "I'm here. Might as well go. How long will the flight be?"

"Air time about 12 hours, sit back and relax. The bar is stocked and the pantry is full. Are you okay traveling alone? I can send Dave back to check on you if you think you might get bored."

"Thanks, but I will be fine. Work to do, you know. The worst thing about modern civilization is that you can't go anywhere to get away from work."

Phil grins and nods his neat blond head in agreement. Then he turns and heads to the cockpit, leaving Rodger alone to speculate on what he is getting himself into. His computer is full of extremely graphic pictures of earlier tsunamis and the aftermath, but they were years ago, and he is certain there has been great progress since then. The problem in communications is something that Phil will work out in flight. Besides there is nothing he can do about it so, he pours himself a drink, belts into his seat, and ponders upon just how that handsome, rascally pilot of his manages to stay single and sober. In the eight years that Phil has worked for Benson Enterprises Rodger has seen him with many an attractive female, but never tipsy. He smiles, and waits till they are airborne before getting back into the work that has been interrupted.

Chapter 2

When he walks back to inform his boss of the anticipated approach to Darwin, Dave expects to find him asleep or hunched over paperwork. Instead, Rodger, freshly shaved, and dressed in clean clothes, offers Dave a newly brewed cup of coffee.

"Trying to take my job," Dave asks, pointing at the coffee.

"Nope, just not on any recognizable schedule. Felt like coffee time." He stands up and hands Dave a cup from the supply cabinet, then nods in the direction of the still full pot. "Help yourself. Does Phil need a shot?"

"Probably, we went through the cockpit's pot a while back, waiting on contact from Darwin. Should come any minute, so strap in."

Rodger nods and returns to the seat. Dave lifts his cup in acknowledgement and returns to his position.

Rodger looks out of the window as the plane banks into its final approach. His eyes see without seeing while his mind marshals the possibilities. Best case scenario, he will land only to find the Bensons were found, safe and are on their way to New York. Then there is a chance the Bensons were found dead and he will need to handle the aftermath, both as friend and COO. Worse case? The Bensons are missing without much hope of recovery. He has a desperate need of information without which little planning can be done. A small bounce of the plane that announces touch down brings him out of his meanderings. He gathers his belongings.

Rodger inclines his head toward his pilots as he deplanes talking into his phone. A car pulls out onto the runway stopping fifty feet or so from the plane. Its driver, a smallish female, walks toward him. Rodger places his hand over the phone raising his eyebrows in inquiry.

"Hello, sir," says the newcomer. Rodger checks her out. A mass of bright red curls peek out from whatever sort of cap she has on her head. She grins; he smiles back at the two dimples making their appearance. Blue eyes match the blue uniform.

"I am from the hotel Northwest in town. I am here to pick up Mr. Rodger Madden?"

"That's me, but I don't have a reservation."

"Uh, yes you do, sir," says Dave. "We called it in about two hours back. We will follow you over there after we secure things here. Thought you might have to set up whatever."

"Hey, this is a nice place, boss. Go with Karen. Want us to check in when we get there?" Phil chimes in.

"Yes, please," Rodger answers, looking between Phil and the young lady. He hopes this will not prove a distraction for the guys. He doesn't have time to play boy scout leader right now.

He is whisked to the hotel and escorted to the penthouse. First order of business is to establish contact with both Amur in Indonesia and James in New York. Working from his laptop, he determines Amur will be a better time fit. He calls but there is no answer. After the sixth try he decides to hell with the time. He dials James, expecting to wake him, but James picks up on the third ring.

"Wish you had told me about your travel plans," James began. "We could have coordinated from here."

"Coordinated?"

"Yes, did you call Amur?"

"Yes, but there was no answer."

"Well, we heard from him by way of a two-way radio. Cell towers are all down in Benkulu and all surrounding areas. The affected area is huge."

"Yeah, okay, but can you get me in there?" Rodger hears the sigh and the fatigue in James' voice.

"I'll tell you what we have come up with. There is no way in or out except by plane or boat."

"Boat?" Rodger interrupts. "I thought this was a tsunami How do boats have access?"

"Because the problem is ashore now, not on the water. The boats can maneuver out at sea; they have problems getting in to shore. The planes have problems finding adequate landing places where they can get permission to land. Most airfields that are cleared enough for planes are only taking official planes or those bringing in supplies. I have taken the liberty of using some of the company's benevolent fund to send a planeload of medical and humanitarian supplies from Sydney to the affected areas. We will put you on board as our company ambassador. At any rate, that is the thought from here. Once there, you will need to find a way to get in touch with Amur. I will provide you with his call numbers, and you can go from there."

"Great job, James, thank you. Do you know when the plane will land and if I can put our pilots in charge?"

"The plane will land there tonight. You should be ready to go first thing tomorrow. I will check on the pilot substitution, but I really don't foresee a problem, it *is* our plane. By the way, I had to put this through over your signature, so I will send the paperwork for you to print and sign."

He smiles. James the legal one, never signs anything if he can avoid it. Safe, that is James. "Hey man, appreciate you. Go get some rest."

Rodger hangs up about the time the knock comes. "Come," he says.

Phil and Dave enter, their briefcases dangling and hats pushed back. Poor guys, they think they are off duty. He purses his lips, "Have one drink fellows and get some rest. First thing tomorrow we head for Indonesia."

Phil grimaces. "Boss, I know you are anxious to get there, but there's no way they are going to let a small private jet take up space."

Rodger tilts his head, "You're right. We will need to take the big plane full of supplies. Check with the office in Sydney see if you are cleared to fly whatever type of plane they have ordered, and make sure you finish whatever you have to do. I know you are tired but to be quite honest, I want you two around in case I need help. I trust you, don't know the guys coming in. Sorry if that messes with your plans, Phil, but I promise some R&R time when this mess is over." He sincerely hopes he will still be in a position to make good on that promise when this thing is over.

He sends down for drinks and printouts of the papers James sent to his computer. Talk is light as three sets of eyes follow the TV news program. What they are seeing is again old pictures of years past mainly the two thousand and four boxing day tsunami. Why no new photos? Surely some pictures or video are available. Shortly after Rodger sends for supper, the three men eat whatever it is that is sent up and then separate. Rodger for a fitful night of sleeping then waking and then sleeping again, while his military trained pilots sleep the sleep of men who know, for tonight, they are safe.

Wednesday begins well. Rodger, Phil, and Dave arrive at the airport in Darwin early to find the plane from Sydney sitting on the tarmac ready to go. Dave heads to inspect the plane while Phil and Rodger go to talk with the officials. Everything is flowing as smoothly as a downhill stream until the passenger manifest rears its ugly head, "Whoa," says Phil. What is this? Four passengers? No, only one, Mr. Madden here."

"Oh no," answers the official. "It says right here, there will be three passengers from Sydney, a doctor and two nurses who will be joined by one passenger here, that would be you Mr. Madden correct? My understanding is that you will all be able to fly to Palembang and unload, then the plane will be required to return here almost immediately. I have the papers of the passengers from Sydney. You, Mr. Godwin, and Mr. Campbell will take the place of the pilots. Now do you and the other passengers intend to stay or return when the plane comes back here?" He turns toward Rodger.

Rodger pauses. As he looks into the passenger area, he sees one man and two women. The doctor and two nurses he thinks. "I haven't had time to confer with the medical team," Rodger says as Phil's eyes go from shock to admiration. "Phil, you stay and answer the er, excuse me, what is your name again?"

"Smythe, William Smythe," smiles the official.

"Yes, of course. Phil answer Mr. Smythe's concerns and let me catch up with our medical team."

He exits the office and intercepts the three individuals. There is a mature woman whose salt and pepper hair and general skin condition place her closer to fifty than he guessed at first glance. Her intelligent eyes twinkle confidently at Rodger's approach. "Hello," she says, holding out her hand. Rodger glances at the younger, albeit taller, dark haired woman who stands calm and silent beside her and the much younger man, twirling an unlit cigarette in his hand, whose deferential air has Rodger readjusting his original opinion.

"Doctor?" asks Rodger taking her extended palm in his.

"Yes, Margarot Burrell. This is Evelyn Hope and Bobby Underwood. We are with Doctor's International and will be working the area. And you are?"

"Rodger Madden. I am COO of Benson Industries. Our plane. What do you know about the situation in Benkulu area? My understanding is that we will land at Palembang, unload, and the plane will have to return here. So we need to determine who will be staying and who will be coming back."

"Well," Margarot grins, "We will be staying, but I strongly suggest you don't even bother taking the flight. I know that you are getting a lot of really good publicity for your company and that it would be enhanced by your presence at the scene, but you can tell everyone you were there and still stay here. You have no idea what you are getting yourself into."

"All things considered, Doctor, you don't know my intentions. I have a good friend with his wife and family somewhere in this mess, as a matter of fact, he isn't only my friend, he is the owner of this company. I need to find them and extract them from the area as soon as possible."

He recognizes the sympathy in the eyes of both ladies as Margarot shakes her head, "Seriously, you have no idea what this is. You should consider staying and waiting here. Meanwhile, when do you think we might board?"

In less that two hours they are on their way. Rodger can't remember being this uncomfortable on a plane. He is accustom to the company jet with lots of space, food, drinks and room. Here there is wall to wall *stuff*, with barely enough space for the four passengers. He can walk to the bathroom if he plans his way carefully. He is seated between the taciturn young man and boxes full of bottles that clink and rattled with every movement. The longer they are in the air the more Rodger resents his entry necessitating the three passengers. He is the one deciding the fate of the plane and its supplies. He should be sitting comfortably close to the cockpit preferably in a first class seat. His irritation grows with the tinkling laughter from the two women sitting in front of him. It is nice to know they are enjoying their ride at his expense. That doctor is part aborigine, he thinks to himself, twisting his mouth in disgust, at least that is her appearance. They should have sent in a competent medical team if they are using his company to get them there. Resentment seethes and he squirms in his seat banging his knees into the back of Margarot's chair as he considers his options.

He glances over at Bobby. He has to be in his twenties, a pimply, wet behind the ears kid with a nicotine addition. The kid managed to smoke on the short stroll to board the plane, and now he sits there with another cigarette tucked behind his ear. He'd probably light up now if Dr. Burrell wasn't aboard. Bobby never looks up from some magazine that he is reading

This is never going to work. When they get on the ground, he will insist they all return. Finally, Rodger dozes off, still plotting his next order. He wakes to hear Dave, talking quietly to the two women. Bobby is still engrossed in his reading. Whatever the article is, it seems much more intriguing to the youngster than what Dave is saying. Rodger rises, stretches, and heads toward the front.

"Hey Boss," says Dave. "I was telling Dr. Burrell we should be cleared for landing soon. They are trying to make a spot for us to put down."

"Be sure to tell them we have refrigerated medications on board so if they can put us as close to a cooler as possible, it would be nice," says Bobby without taking his eyes off the page.

Rodger glances back startled. Evidently, Bobby can multitask. Dave grins and returns to the cockpit. Rodger waits until Dave leaves and the group is down to those who are penciled to stay before he begins his little talk. "I have been thinking it over, and I really feel that you three should remain on board, and, as soon as they get this plane unloaded, head back to Australia. You could wait till things are bit more settled before you try to establish a mission."

A huge sigh escapes Margarot while a tiny giggle emanates from Evelyn. Margarot turns to Rodger and, with a twinkle of a grin teasing the corner of her mouth, asks, "Mr. Madden, who do you think is going to unload this plane?"

"The airport personal will surely get that done."

Evelyn simpers, "Nah, sir. There won't be anyone to help. It's sort of our job, you see."

No, he doesn't see. Executive plane owners, doctors, nurses, and whatever the hell Bobby Underwood's title is, don't empty planes. That is out of the question. He stands still, challenging the statement that hangs in the air like a scream of fire in a theater.

"Welcome to the real world, Mr. Madden. Did you bring your work clothes?" Margarot shakes her head. "You see why I say you need to leave? Look, no worries, you had nothing to help you understand what you are headed toward. No one will think less of you if you head back and await news of your friends from a safer place."

Rodger's brain races through options. His number one objective, find some Benson family member alive. And for that reason, all other problems fade into trivia. The company must be protected at all cost. Deep breath, set mouth, informs the remaining company that the appeal is getting no consideration.

Oh well, Margarot shrugs, she tried. "Look if we are going to be hauling cargo and tromping around in hell, we might as well get to first name basis. I can't keep shouting Mr. Madden every time I need your attention." She extends her hand as if they had never met and says, "Maggie."

He hesitates, takes her hand and with a rye twist of his lips answers, "Rodger."

"Good," comments the bored voice of Bobby. "I was betting he would say Mr. Madden. Then what ever would you do Maggs?"

"Stuff yourself," Maggie replies. "Evelyn, any comments?"

The quiet young nurse extends her hand to Rodger, "Welcome to the team Rodger. Good luck on your quest."

They retake their seats as Phil's voice announces eminent landing. Smiles are replaced by grim facades as the four in the cabin remember their missions.

The Wave Effect 17

Chapter 3

The plane touches down with a bump and a jerk, leading someone in the cabin to emit a few well chosen oaths. As soon as they are into taxi mode, Maggie is up checking on her precious supplies, as she hangs on to the seat with her off hand. The rest look curiously out the windows. The airport looks to be fairly well maintained, albeit old and small. The buildings have some roof damage and there is excess water along the edges of the runways. Rodger is puzzled. The Tsunami was miles from here, along the opposite coast. Despite that, it appears as if its damage extends even this far inland. Evelyn's sharp intake of breath, and Bobby's sudden interest in his surroundings gives Rodger the distinct feeling that he is not the only one surprised at the view.

The plane slides to a stop. Phil comes forward and opens the door. There are people all about scurrying around the various planes and buildings, but no one approaches their aircraft. Phil reaches into some hidden compartment and produces a rope ladder which he flings out of the door and promptly scampers down. He walks to the nearest building while Rodger stands in shock. He doesn't mind going down the ladder, but carrying boxes down is not a good idea in any kind of world. Busy contemplating the many ways one might be able to get the boxes inside the plane to the tarmac, he is startled when he is abruptly shoved aside. "Move over Rodger," Maggie sings out. "Bobby, you are with me, Evelyn, you and Rodger check to make sure all the boxes containing the medicines that are sensitive to the heat are clearly marked. We will be taking that out last, I think. Depends on what equipment they have."

Rodger steps back as Bobby scampers down the ladder after Maggie. It strikes him how much cooler inside the aircraft is than the outside.

Evelyn pokes his arm to get his attention. "Come on," she says. "This part is easy. We are looking at the tape sealing the boxes. If it is yellow, that box is sensitive to heat. Any other color and it is good to go. Let's make sure all the yellow boxes are on the left side of the aisle and all the rest are, wait, no, let's get the other boxes to the rear of the plane."

"How? What?" Rodger is lost.

Evelyn smiles and explains, "Move all the boxes without the yellow tape to the rear of the plane. Don't know if they will be last or first but they will all go together. We need to move as quickly as possible."

Rodger frowns but, following her lead, he begins to separate the cargo. While they are sorting, Dave enters the cabin only to make his way down to the hold of the plane. Rodger notices a wagon coming along side the aircraft and more boxes passing from the inside storage to be stacked onto the wagon. Most of the yellow marked boxes are now in the front third of the passenger compartment.

Rodger steps to the door and looks out. The view is varied and fascinating. Hangers and aluminum storage buildings shimmer in the bright sun. Further back sit block buildings that might house passengers or airport business offices. A tropical forest comes right up to the edge of the asphalt runway. Above the trees, Rodger spies a thin stream of smoke, but over all, this place isn't much different from a small airport in south Florida that is under repair.

He is hot. Sweat clings to his skin like a thin mist. The air outside the plane feels like a blanket of steam. His light blue silk shirt has sweat circles under both arms; it will never be the same, a tosser for sure. It is difficult to breathe, and though he is inside, working under these conditions will be hard.

But it isn't what he sees or how he feels that has him nailed to the door of that plane. It is that *smell*. He can't put a name to the odor, yet it seems vaguely familiar. Whatever created that smell, it is not anything he knows or wishes to know. The stench crawls inside his nose, it makes its way down his throat coating every particle of his mouth, nose, tongue. He can almost taste it. It replaces all the good and gentle odors that have lived forever in his memory bank. Where were all the flowers, the sweet shrubs that surely live only inches below those trees? Why can't he smell them, and just what is this? It comes and goes on the breeze making him think it is right here then no, it is over there. His body craves the breeze that brings the cooling and dreads it all at the same time.

Evelyn notices his inaction and quickly drags his attention back to the task at hand. When they have all the cargo separated, Maggie yells up at them, "Get the back door open."

Rodger shakes his head. Of course, they will send the boxes down the chute and load from there. He looks for the lever to activate the chute when he sees a hustling Maggie, Bobby with a cigarette dangling from his mouth, and Phil busily setting two long boards with hooks on the ends at the rear door. Once the boards are lifted so the hooks face the plane entrance, he helps Evelyn grab them, placing the hooks firmly in the entrance. Evelyn begins pushing box after box down the poles. Rodger prepares to help when Maggie tells him to go start the same procedure at the front door. There is a closed cart by that door and as soon as the two poles are in place, he begins sliding the sensitive medical supplies toward Phil and another man on the ground. In a half hour, the plane is completely empty. Rodger and Evelyn secure the back door and climb down joining those already on the ground.

When all supplies are on the appropriate carts, Phil and Dave begin preparing the craft for take off. As he boards, Phil stops and asks, "Did anyone think to bring food?"

Four faces look wonderingly at each other. "I take it that's a no?" Phil smiles, "Fortunately, Dave never goes anywhere without food, holdover from his combat days I suspect. Get the boxes man, we can't leave them here like this. Sure you don't want to go back with us?"

Dave drops three large boxes down, Bobby catches the first one, Rodger staggers but manages to corral the second, and the islander, one of those who helped them unload, gets the third. The group stands there watching the door to their escape closing, each feels the sucking pull of panic. Rodger desperately wants to beat on the side of the plane until one of the guys opens the door for him, but he can't. There is work to be done. He will never know how much his desire is shared by the rest.

Olgur, the Indonesian, is introduced. He shakes every hand thanking each profusely for coming. Rodger gathers the man speaks

The Wave Effect 21

little English. Maggie, fortunately, speaks a little Indonesian. Between them plus a lot of hand gestures, the group understands they need to vacate the runway and head to the building where a few other men are taking the carts. Once the carts clear the tarmac, their plane engines begin to fire. Maggie sighs, "Well, phase one down, lets get to work folks."

Rodger follows along trying his best to figure out where he should go from here, and how he will get there. Somehow that part of the planning escaped his attention. He is here, he needs to be there, but nothing looks in anyway familiar. And that smell again, he cannot shake it or banish it from his senses. He steps up beside Bobby to ask, "What is that odor?"

Bobby glances at Rodger's face, "Burning flesh".

Rodger's eyes jerk upward, "What? No, no way man. Why?" His head will not accept it, his hands begin to shake.

"Look, there has been a lot of death here, both animals as well as human. They can't leave the carcasses to rot, not in this heat and humidity, there would be all sorts of nasty germs incubating. I know it is hard to imagine, but it is for the best."

Maggie drops back beside them, "Worse, there was a big storm only hours after the tsunami so more vegetation is down, meaning there are more roads that are closed. All that means fewer helpers, and fewer supplies. The government is working on providing for the living, they can't take the time to properly honor the dead. Welcome to hell, Rodger. I did tell you."

He stares at the path taken by the plane, his plane. With his face bleached white, his lips pressed firmly together to prevent him from retching, Rodger considers the insanity of his position and wonders at his stubborn nature.

Chapter 4

Four hours. Four *fucking* hours on this road and he still sees the airport. They are a party of seven, the Indonesian driver, Olgur, a soldier, Rodger, and the medical team. While the driver fights to keep the ancient vehicle on what used to be a road, the rest take turns riding in the dilapidated troop convoy with the supplies or walking ahead to remove debris. One would think nothing has moved down this road in years, but obviously other vehicles have even today.

His shirt is now covered with a white film that could only mean he is losing a lot of salt. He would gladly swap a month's salary plus his five-hundred-dollar pair of Armondo shoes for Olgur's sneakers. The nice but serviceable pants he chose are anything but. They contain three tears already as well as the inevitable sweat marks. Rodger shakes his head; he's brought along a small bag with two changes of underwear and two extra shirts, and nothing else.

He loses all concern about body odor three hours into this ordeal. The only compensation is that the others smell as badly as he, although they are better prepared as to clothing and other necessities. Oh well, he will purchase a few items when they get to their destination *if* they ever do.

Maggie taps him on the shoulder, nodding toward the truck. "Your turn to ride for a bit," she says with a smile.

Rodger wants to knock that smile right off her face. He wants to refuse to ride while she walks, but he can't summon the energy to do either. He glumly takes a seat and watches as Maggie joins the soldier Ali, and Omar, the second worker, clearing the road. Inside the vehicle quiet reigns. Everyone is drained.

"How much longer to Benkulu?"

"At our present rate, I'd estimate eight to twelve more hours. We might pick up speed a bit if we get past the tropical storm damage and before we get to the tsunami area," Bobby says.

As he finishes speaking, they hear an engine. Four heads peek out around the back end of the truck. They see nothing but there is a cheer going up. Maggie appears and jumps onto the back of the truck. "Another crew is clearing from the other direction. We are all going to get to ride for a while, And they have some extra petrol!"

"Is gas a problem?" asks Rodger.

"Of course." answers Evelyn. "Always is in a disaster."

He again feels the inadequacy of information. The two fellows jump into the cab, and they are off. "Wow, we must be doing at least eight to ten miles per hours. We will be there in no time." His mouth turns upward as he glances at the rest of the crew.

No one else in the back of the truck is considering when they will arrive, they are all making themselves as comfortable as possible preparing to gather whatever rest they can. He watches, then follows suit. He is shocked when their abrupt stop awakens him. It is dark, there is no light to focus on, and the smell that haunted him all day is stronger. The rest of the party are outside discussing food. It appears they are stopped for the night. He steps out, still exhausted, and joins the group without a word. He tries to eat, and he listens.

It is afternoon of the next day before the reality of the tsunami comes into view. They have been traveling through destruction all along but nothing like this. First thing Rodger notices is a boat sitting on top of a crushed house both oozing water. The boat doesn't look harmed, only out of place. The trees drip with all sorts of odd and unusual stuff. There is an old fashion push mower hanging in one tree, below that is some kind of being, whether animal or human Rodger can't tell.

That smell is now so prominent that his nostrils seem to have acquired an immunity. He doesn't know if that is a good thing or bad. Maybe the smell will be with him forever. Maybe he will never know the sweet smell of a spray of lilies or the clean odor of a freshly laundered shirt. At least he has stopped throwing up everything he puts in his mouth. As they travel closer to the coast, the more the horrible becomes the ordinary. Metal spikes driven through crumbled buildings, bits of clothing hanging from limbs ripped from trees that are now sideways in sloshy collections of trash. Stacks of rubble are everywhere, here an arm still grasps a metal studding that is bent away from the coast toward the hills beyond. It is as if they have wandered into the world's largest garbage dump with nothing off limits. Boats, half boats, building materials, foliage, broken pottery, automobiles, trucks, whole sheds stand rotting in the heat and humidity beside a small cloth doll not damaged at all and a watch that hangs from a piece of rebar. Pile upon pile of everything known to man with no order, no limit, only chaos as far as the eye can see. Empty shells, once fine hotels, still hang together enough that one can make out their original purpose, no one inside them, nothing left of grand lobbies, dining rooms, spacious bars. He assumes that somewhere the swimming pools still exist although they are now covered by the hideous mound of waste. He wonders if rescuers ever consider that the mess they are standing on could be the center of a pool. Would it matter if they did?

Rodger's first thought is how does anyone survive this. His second is how will he find anyone in this. Maggie was right - welcome to hell.

As they approached the city that had been Benkulu, the vehicle slows even more. Here and there up on the massive stockpile of jetsam, Rodger can see figures picking through the rubble, some with tools but most bare-handed. A roar goes up and someone pulls a body from beneath a pile of something that once housed human beings. Quickly the body is laid on a sheet and the four men hurry toward a destination.

"Follow that group there," orders Dr. Burrell. "They will be headed to whatever answers for a hospital here."

Rodger wants to protest that they need to look for a hotel or some place to stay, but is glad he didn't when the next turn in the road brings even more disaster with almost no standing buildings at all. If someone bombed this place, he thinks, it wouldn't look this bad. It seems to him that anywhere there is anything standing is a miracle. He has seen pictures, not reality. Reality is tough to digest.

The simplest of tasks seem impossible. The first question, where to start, seems unanswerable. What to do? Where to begin? He is lost and for the first time in his memory, Rodger Madden feels totally incompetent. He awaits orders from a woman while he soaks in sights and sounds that he isn't prepared for, the total destruction he hasn't considered. His plan, which included a competent hotel, purchasing a better pair of shoes and new pants is a fantasy. Whatever lies ahead, one thing is certain. Rodger Madden will never forget what he is seeing. Or that smell.

Picking their way inch by inch, the team tries to follow the gurney ahead, but the rescuers are on foot, not hauling a truck load of supplies that are far too valuable to leave the roadside. Maggie can't wait. She bolts out of the truck and chases after the group on foot. While Rodger is stunned into inactivity, Bobby heads after Maggie, shouting, "Come on Maggs, wait on me." The truck grounds to a standstill and everyone else tries as best they can to follow with their eyes. Bobby lets out a whistle and points. The driver picks his way in the general direction of that now disappeared finger. The way gets perceptively more difficult as the crush of trash caused by the wave stacks upon anything that stopped it. Trees and trash mingle with crushed buildings and bodies. In one place, there stands a house with a what appears to be a dog's house on top of it, the dog still attached, though no longer a part of this place or this world. Rodger registers it all as the truck grounds to yet another stop.

This time it is met by a group of workers, who begin unloading the boxes and carrying them away toward whatever lies beyond that corner. He grabs a box and joins the procession, heading who knows where, but hopefully somewhere better than here.

A small warehouse building, miraculously still intact comes into view. Maggie hustles out to greet them and to explain where the boxes need to go. There is a tiny fan which to Rodger's amazement is turning, cooling the building down at least a fraction. Maggie notices his look and comments with a twist of her head, "Generator."

Little by little and mostly by hand, the contents of the truck join the contents of the clinic, as he deems it. Inside are as many bodies as could be crammed into the tiny space. There are three males that seem to be heading up the operation of this makeshift hospital. One of them is telling everyone where to put the supplies and making sure that those precious heat sensitive medications are stored as close to the fan as possible, although Rodger can't see how it could possibly matter as the heat is so totally oppressive. Maggie dives right in helping the victims, while Bobby works on storing the supplies, and Evelyn assists filling out paperwork on the victims along with the other medical personal.

"They have done this before," thinks Rodger with a bit of surprise. He never took this team for anything but his ruse to get close to the main disaster area, never considered their actual utility. He is inconveniently in the way. He takes his turn unloading supplies then wanders out to discover a form of communication. The enormity of the affected area gives him pause. Can he find a way out for himself, much less for anyone else? He checks his cell phone mostly out of habit. No signal, what a shock. In the back of the building, he discovers an old fashion, wind-up two-way radio. Remembering that he has Amur's call signal in this back pocket, he pulls it out and asks the gentleman working in the room if he can use the radio. In minutes, he is talking to Amur, who is on a boat somewhere off the main beach which is only blocks away. He explains his situation, and sets up a meeting place, then goes inside to find Maggie. She is, as he had expected, working with a victim. The bruises that cover the body and face of the person on that bed make him ache. He avoids making eye contact with the groaning human. Instead he informs Maggie where he is going and how she can get in touch with him. She is too busy to take down his information but sends him to Evelyn. He gives his information to Evelyn, leaves the care facility, and walks toward relief.

Carefully picking his way between the flotsam and crumbling ruins of the town and waterfront, he makes his way to the area that once was a gorgeous beach. He keeps his head down to prevent the misstep that would send him back to the makeshift hospital he just left, therefore, he doesn't see Amur walking toward him until a voice nearby says, "Welcome to Indonesia."

He looks up at the smiling man and feels the relief all the way to his poorly shod toes. "Man," Rodger shakes his head, "I am so glad to see a familiar, English-speaking face."

Amur grins and gestures back from where he had come. "Your yacht awaits my liege."

"This has been extremely hard to process," says Rodger as he falls in step beside the dark haired head of security for Benson Enterprises Mideast."Some how, it seemed much more manageable before I actually saw this." He sweeps his hand crosswise to include all of what is gathered on the beach. He stops and looks inland. He has traveled across all this for the last two days but now, seeing it from the edge of the beach inward, it is somehow different. He is overwhelmed. He remembered as a child squirting a fierce flow of water toward a driveway to clear it off. This looks like an Angel has cleared or cleaned every ocean and land therein and pushed all the castaway trash here, then left it. Again and again, Rodger shakes his head, trying and failing to process what he is witnessing. It is too much.

Chapter 5

Rodger's first requirement upon boarding the yacht is a bath and a change of clothes. He revels in the luxury of hot clean water. Amur earns bonus points as he provides his boss with clean clothes that he brought aboard guessing the situation. Rodger heads to the deck where the two men are served cocktails and snacks, and then left alone to discuss the past few days.

"I found the Bensons, at least Carl and Maria. So far no sign of Annalisel," Amur begins. "Carl and Maria died on the balcony of the hotel. The maid who serviced their room survived. She says she thinks they were sleeping when the wave came ashore. I have learned that this wave was so much faster than anything anyone has seen If you didn't move immediately, you were caught."

"You talked to this maid? Correct?"

"Yes,"

"Do you know where she is now?"

"No, but I will find out. I suspect she is staying on the top floor of the hotel. As unsafe as that sounds, it is where the staff is housed and I dare say she has nowhere else to go. Why?"

"We need to talk with her and see what we can find out about the daughter. To put it to you bluntly, if you like working for this company, we need that girl to keep the company from going to auction and all proceeds going to Carl's favorite charities." Rodger grimaces as he relates their shared predicament. "Myself, I am looking for any clue. By the way, did you actually see the remains? I mean are you very sure the Bensons are deceased?"

"Unfortunately, yes. I had their bodies brought aboard. They are down in the hold."

"What? Why? I mean what are we going to do with them, we can't let them... " Rodger stops speaking as his olfactory nerves recreate the smell that followed him across Indonesia.

"The bodies are refrigerated. And I plan to take then across to Jakarta to be flown to the states. As a matter of fact, we were preparing to pull out when I got your call. So, what do you want to do next?"

Rodger pauses to consider the situation. He takes a deep breath and begins to sort out the requisite actions that need to occur and their probable order. "You are right. We need to get the bodies back to the states as soon as possible. Meanwhile someone needs to continue the search for Annalisel. I would like to talk with the maid. Do you know her name? And I think I should ask Dr. Burrell to be on the lookout for anyone matching Anna's description. When was the last time you saw her?"

"Anna or the maid, Naydar?"

"Anna, and what did you say the name is?"

"Naydar. I talked with her yesterday," Amur shakes his head. "I haven't seen Annalisel since she was a child. You?"

"I saw her last Christmas, but I didn't pay any attention to her. She's a kid for Pete's sake. I have no idea if I could recognize her or not." Rodger shakes his head and fumbles with his cocktail. "If we find her, how would we go about proving it is her?"

"The authorities will take her word, they have too many unconscious bodies to waste resources. If she is unable to speak, they will want a fingerprint match to her birth prints. She was born in the U.S. right?" At Rodger's nod, he continues, "Or her passport if that could be found."

Rodger pauses in his pacing looks at Amur sighs and says, "Okay I am going back ashore to try and talk with Dr. Burrell and the maid. Meanwhile you get things ready to move and as soon as I return we are headed to Jakarta. If you can get a message out, warn James and have someone ready to receive the bodies. We will plan the funeral when I can get there. Tell him to contact the company plane, have them ready to take off as soon as we get the bodies to them."

Amur nods, "Why don't I go on and take the bodies, I can be back here by tomorrow and we can start our search for the girl as soon as I get back. I'll talk to James about the passport or other items we might need to provide ID."

Rodger considers the possibilities then agrees. The galley staff comes above with lunch and the two eat in silence each thinking of the next few hours. As soon as lunch is over, Rodger asks that all available food reserves that can fit into a basket be packed. He then orders Amur to fill the boat with whatever medical supplies and food that it can safely transport for the return trip. Taking his basket of food as a peace offering, he steps ashore and once more watches as his escape vehicle vanishes. This is not something he wishes to become habitual.

He stops, looks around to set his retreat. He sees nothing of interest except the rescue workers digging through debris. One would think there would be more of them, he ponders. He scans the horizon for any sign of the resort that housed the Bensons. Trouble is he sees only shells, not buildings. It might have been easy if he had a view from a week ago. He could have picked out Carl's preference, but now? There are a few structures that at least partially remain. Amur said the maid was in an upper level still standing. He looks around. There are three structures that might qualify; one is pink, one sand colored, one white. Okay. Considering his options, he decides to investigate the middle hotel. If he finds the maid, Naydar, they can talk and he will be on his way to the clinic and a redress with Maggie the Mighty.

Rodger picks his way between broken and breaking steps conscious of each move he makes. He is on unsure and unsteady ground. Each step that leads toward the upper levels and his target seem less and less secure. Each floor is dryer and less compromised that the previous one, however, the problem is that the base on which these floors depend is desperately stressed. His heart rate increases as he climbs, not from exertion. He hears a whisper and a giggle. Around the corner, a face peaks out at him. He smiles, "Hello. Naydar?" He really doesn't expect a positive answer, but hopes for an introduction. Instead, the giggler drops her dark eyes and nods. She appears all of ten or twelve years old, short, and slight of build, not the sturdy stock that his mind associates with a cleaning staff. A small cute sprite, she is. "Do you speak English?" Again her head bobs, the eyes dart up to him and return to the floor. She holds up one hand with the thumb and first finger indicating a small amount.

"Do you know the Bensons?" He drags words out increasing the volume as if that will somehow make what he is saying more intelligible.

"Mem and Sab Benson? Yes. So sorry," her face easy to read.

He nods, "And Annalisel?"

She shrugs, again the face too easily read.

They look at each other in frustration. He should have waited for Amur. He smiles, opens the basket and gives her half of the food, saving the rest until he sees her inhaling her potion. He shrugs, takes a bit for later, and hands the basket to the hungry girl.

"I'll need to talk to you soon, okay?"

She nods, smiles, holds out her hand. He isn't sure she understands his words but he establishes a connection. "Good," he thinks, she will be anxious to help if she feels indebted. Oddly, his load is lighter than a mere basket.

Chapter 6

The medical clinic, or whatever you'd call this place, has not changed since this morning. Still he approaches it with care. No one stops, no one speaks, no one pays any attention to him at all. Inside hasn't changed either. Broken bodies occupy every available space. Evelyn, pad in hand, sits beside a bed taking down answers to questions she asks with the aid of an army officer serving as an interpreter.

Over in the one corner, Bobby inserts a line into the arm of another victim. In another corner of the room, Maggie bends over a cot on which a body lies. There must be life or Maggie would not be wasting her time, but Rodger can't describe the person on that cot. Male? Female? Short? Tall? Awake? Asleep? All he sees is a bruised, broken, still soul with Maggie's hands running all over it.

"New one?" asks Rodger.

Maggie glances sideways at him then returns her attention to her patient. "Yep. Brought in by boat this afternoon. Three fishermen found her caught in a treetop floating on the flotsam. No idea who she is, but I've a long way to go on her." Maggie clucks her tongue, "Oooh What have we here? A ring," she answers herself. Sliding it bit by bit from the limp finger, she places it in a plastic glove she pulls from her pocket and tacks it to the bed. "Possible broken left ulna, two broken phalanges on left hand, possibly more. We really need to get an x-ray machine. I am tired of guessing." She mumbles as she continues to work.

"How do you find out who she is?" Rodger tries to appear disinterested.

"Wait till she wakes up and tells us? I have no idea. Not my field. I thought you left."

"Well, I need to talk with you. There is a young lady about eighteen or nineteen that is missing. Her name is Annalisel Benson. She is the daughter of my boss, and I need to find her ASAP."

"ASAP? Why are you looking for her and not her parents?"

"They are dead, identified and on the way to meet Phil and Dave in Jakarta."

"Oh." She has yet to look at him after that first quick glance. "Poor thing. This girl fits your age parameters, but we will have to wait for her to awaken. We gave her pain meds as soon as we saw her condition."

"Do you think I could talk with the guys who brought her in?" he asks.

"If anyone knows who they are, you might. Look, these guys are working their tails off. They go out, search, bring in anyone they find, and head right back out there. Today they brought me her and three dead bodies. I am already tired of dealing with death, and I have only been here one full day." Maggie shakes her head and the curly salt and pepper hair goes flying.

Rodger stares. She seems so strong, but there are cracks.

She sighs. "So Mr. Madden, what brings you back this way?"

"I wanted to tell you about the girl and ask, no plead with you to be on the look out for anyone fitting her description so we might get her out of here as soon as possible."

"Ah, ASAP. Right, well, this, so far, is all I have and I can't make any identification. She didn't have anything on her and I do mean anything."

"Nothing? No clothes? You mean she was naked?"

"As a yard dog," answers Maggie. "That must have been some kind of wave. Part of me wishes I'd seen it, part of me is delighted I didn't."

"So, how do you identify someone?"

"Well, if they are awake and coherent, or by fingerprint, or DNA, I think? I really don't know. As I said, not my area of expertise. How are you going to get back?"

"The boat will be back tomorrow. They will be bringing more supplies and extra food. If you want, I'll see if they can find a portable x-ray for you."

Maggie beams at him, "Oh yes, if you can."

Rodger nods, "Can I bunk in here tonight?"

"Not in, but Bobby might lend you a blanket for out," answers Maggie.

He gets the message, hanging out with Maggie is a no no. So after his call to Amur from the generator room, Rodger spends his entire afternoon running errands, emptying body wastes, and removing soiled sheets that local women would take to the water's edge to rinse in the brown, trash filled ocean that laps only yards away. How this building survived is either a miracle, or a mystery, or both. Filth is considered by degree. By dark he is exhausted. Ignoring the sarcastic grin on Bobby's face, he takes the offered blanket, sacks out on the mud covered ground, lets the last three days kick in and surprise, surprise, he sleeps.

Chapter 7

Rodger shakes off the bonds of sleep. He staggers as he attempts to stand, his fifty year old knees aching. His knees haven't hurt like this since he stopped running marathons. He feels the urge and looks for a place to relive himself. Up against the wall that once was a part of a building next to this one seems to suffice. How can one dwelling be so totally destroyed and the next not? Unfathomable! He heads inside looking for Bobby whom he discovers in the generator room which also houses all the clinic's food reserves.

"Breakfast?" Bobby asks as he extends a pack of nutritious, tasteless, goop.

Rodger grins, swallows the offering then remembers reinforcements should be already here. "This is all we have?"

"No. But I really like jerking your chain"

"Um, well, while you are playing jokes, might I use the radio?" Bobby gestures toward the equipment. Rodger reaches in his shirt pocket for the number Amur left him. Soon the connection is made. He is informed that Amur is on the way back with food and medicine. "What about the ID of Annalisel, Have you determined what.. "

Amur stops him mid sentence, "Got it covered,boss. No problem. Trust me. Where will you send her when we find her?"

"If we find her," corrects Rodger. "Most likely place will be the estate in upstate New York. There are several employees that have been with the family forever, they will take care of her."

"Right, look, I'll be there in a few. Meanwhile stay put and stay safe."

"Yeah, will do."

It is mid-afternoon when the company's sailors appear at the clinic with boxes of medications, food, and Maggie's x-ray machine. Maggie is beside herself. She starts barking orders before the machine is out of the box. Jane Doe is the first patient under the scope. Meanwhile, everyone else falls in to hump supplies from boat to building. Amur is not among the crew. When Rodger asks, the young sailor shrugs, touches his lips, and smiles. It is almost two more hours before Amur shows up with the maid Naydar in tow.

"So, lets have a look at this unknown girl. See if Naydar knows her." Amur takes the lead. The young maid tiptoes to the bed. She examines the broken body on the cot, purses her lips and wells up. Tears trickle down her face as she turns toward Amur and Rodger, "Yes," she says, "This is Miss Anna."

"Would you stay here with her, clean her up a bit, and sort of watch over her? We will pay you your salary," says Amur.

The girl agrees. She moves beside the cot and gently she touches the face of the patient with as clean a cloth as there is to be had. Amur stops her arm and swaps the not so clean rag with a pristine handkerchief. Naydar drops her eyes and resumes her careful face cleansing. Then she takes a brush from her apron, using the smallest amount of pressure she can, she begins to comb the girl's hair. Again Amur stops her. He says something in the native language as he removes the brush from her hand.

Maggie hurries over. "Whoa! Careful! We have no idea how many broken bones she might have. Here, what I need you to do is sit here, wipe her face when needed, maybe you could keep her lips moist?"

The officer following Maggie translates as she speaks. Naydar replies and sits. She folds her hands in her lap as she assumes her role as caretaker.

"What if this isn't your girl?" asks Maggie.

"Then we will have paid for special care for someone we don't know. However, she says this is Anna," replies Rodger. "We will leave her here in good company and go to the boat. If you think of anything tonight let us know. We will be traveling back and forth to check in on her." And with that Amur and Rodger exit the clinic.

Back at the boat, it is conference and cocktail time. Rodger listens as Amur reports his activities of the day. "Delivered the bodies to the authorities for official death certifications. They are so overwhelmed we had to wait. I left the bodies with two of our guys there, checked to see what types of I.D. the Indonesian government requires. James is checking for whatever documentation that the U.S. will require, and, of course, he is searching for the will of Carl Benson and Maria Benson. I think we need to see what it will take to declare this girl Annalisel Benson."

"What if she isn't?" Rodger swirls the drink in his glass.

"If we prove she is, the authorities will stop looking," argues Amur. "We can look for the proof we need and go backward with it."

Rodger sits in silence as he indicates Amur should continue.

"If you start in the U.S. and Switzerland and head here, the evidence might confirm her or deny her. Think. Suppose we start here and take the proof backward, then we will know the I.D. will match."

"We need a conference call."

Amur raises his eyebrows. "The more people in on this, the more danger there is. That is if you want to continue control of the company." He continues with a sigh, "She is what, eighteen? If that is Annalisel Benson what if she decides she wants to control Benson Enterprises? She could put us out on the street right?"

Rodger looks down at his shoes. He needs a bath, new clothes, food, and some ideas that don't hurt his head. "Yes, she could, but she is hardly prepared to take over the business."

"Yeah, I know that. You know that. But how sure are you that she knows that?"

"All of this is moot until she wakes up."

"Well, we need to get the ball rolling now, then when/if she gains consciousness, we are ready. Come on, let's head to Jakarta. Allow me to set us up."

"Set up what? What are you planning." Rodger looks at Amur in frustration.

Amur's grin resembles a leer. He twirls his ring. "Leave it to me. I'll get everything in motion. Trust me, you are better off not knowing. We can make Jakarta and be back here tomorrow. I'll stay there and start the wheels going."

"Nope, I'm not staying outside again, I need to be here close to the girl." Mind racing, Rodger paces the deck.

"No problem, I'll hire another boat to take me. The air strip should be cleared by next week. Now, we can get in and out with less security, less questions. I agree it would be great if someone were there when the girl regains consciousness. Naydar is a great girl and all, but you know, if one of us is there we can better direct things."

Rodger isn't sure where this is leading, but at the moment, he is too upset to consider the innuendoes. Amur is a trusted employee. Carl trusted him. James, good ole by the book James, recommended him, for God's sake. Something tries to slide through Rodger's mind. He tries to focus, but it isn't working. *Let it go*, he tells himself.

Amur calls someone on his radio, bids farewell to Rodger and hops off the boat. He takes a small bag with him as he heads toward another boat anchored two hundred feet away. "See you soon, boss!" he calls over his shoulder as he walks away.

"Keep me posted," Rodger shouts after him, although he isn't sure he wants to be updated on Amur's plans. What he wants, what he needs, is for that girl in Maggie's clinic to wake up, perk up, and declare to the world that she is Annalisel Benson. Oh Lord, please let her.

Chapter 8

Rodger is back at the mission clinic early the following morning. Naydar sits beside the young girl's bedside, quiet and still. Maggie is three cots down, out of ear shot. He smiles at Naydar, points to the girl on the cot, and lifts an eyebrow in question.

Naydar speaks, "She has quiet night, sir. She uh, try to awake."

He struggles with his lack of communication and looks around for one of the interpreters. Not seeing anyone, he points to Naydar and indicates that she can leave, he will sit for a while. Naydar starts to protest, then nods. She leaves the two alone. Rodger examines the girls features, willing her to bring back a memory, a sense of connection, but it has been too long, and, to his regret, he paid too little attention when last they met. She stirs, he inhales and holds his breath, wishing, praying for an awaking. She sighs. Sleep returns.

Maggie makes her way over. "She is doing great," she says. "I expect her to wake up any moment. You understand we must be gentle with her when she awakens?"

He nods. "Has anyone else been discovered?"

"Yes, we had three more brought in last night. They are all barely alive, hanging on. We are praying, but they are edgers."

"Edgers?"

"Well," answers Maggie, "In any disaster like this one, there is a time line. Usually three to four days max to find survivors. After that any surviving is a miracle and most of your duty becomes tagging, recording, and disposing of the dead. This is not an easy or enjoyable situation, but it is what it is. You hope. You pray. You continue to work, and once in a great while the miracle happens." She pats him on the shoulder and bends over her patient. Rodger has no idea when the lady sleeps, for she has been on duty every moment he has been anywhere near.

The girl sighs. Maggie's face splits into a grin big enough to fill the room. "Won't be long now," she comments as she moves to the next cot.

Evelyn walks up with her book. "Do you know her?"

"I think so; I hope so. It has been too long since I saw her for me to be sure. We are waiting for her to regain consciousness."

"I think it will be soon. She is so much better today than yesterday. Where is the girl who was sitting with her?"

He shrugs. Evelyn purses her lips. "Maybe she knows more. When the interpreter gets here, I'll see he stops by. Do you know where her people are?"

"No, I only met her yesterday. She worked at the hotel and was staying in the upper floors."

"Good thing you got her out," says Evelyn.

"Why?"

"You didn't hear? That place collapsed this morning. Why the sound of it woke me up. Glad she wasn't there."

"What about the ones who were?" he asks as images of streaked faces slipped through his brain.

"We got three dead and one wounded here. Don't know how many there were," she answers.

He pulls at his shirt collar and runs shaky fingers through his hair. "When does it end?"

"When it ends," she sighs and walks away.

He checks it out. Everything is the same. Everywhere there is the sound of murmurs interrupted by groans, the smell of medication, and vomit. The heat is oppressive and the boredom unrelieved. He falls asleep.

"Where is this? Who are you? Ooh," groans the girl on the bed. Rodger snaps to attention. Naydar jumps up from the opposite side of the bed.

"Miss Anna, you alright?" Nadyar claps. Rodger tenses.

"Who? Who are you? Where? What? My arm ooh." She groans through purple swollen lips that stand out even among the black bruises on her face.

"Dr. Maggie, she awake." Naydar's voice blares out in the quiet room. "Come, come."

Maggie bustles over with Bobby on her heels. The girl's eyes are huge and lost. Her head flops from side to side as she takes in bit by bit the atmosphere that surrounds her. The tiny area she views has twelve people in various stages of injury. There are three other workers besides Maggie and Bobby, and one extra visitor besides Rodger and Naydar. The space is crowded. The silence, broken by the girl and filled by the people surrounding her bed, returns.

"Hello, I am Dr. Burrell, Maggie. You have been injured in a Tsunami. You are in a medical unit where we are treating your injuries." Rodger pokes Maggie's shoulder. "Would you tell me your name?"

"My name is," she stops, "I'm er," The eyes go huge again. "I don't know who I am? I don't know!" She begins to weep. She raises her hand toward her face, then screams in agony.

Maggie stops the arm in mid path leading it back to its position on the bed. "Your arm is broken as are several of your fingers. Your body is badly bruised. Do you remember what happened?"

"No, I... I... I..." The girl's tears drip down her cheeks onto what passes for a pillow.

"What is the last thing you remember?" Maggie prods.

"I don't... I woke up here. Nothing, Oh my God, nothing."

"Shush," soothes Naydar. "Shush."

Maggie whispers something to Bobby who disappears into the radio room. He hustles back with a full syringe in hand. Maggie thanks him, takes the needle, and injects the girl.

"Ouch," The girl stiffens, then as the meds take effect, she relaxes into a quiet slumber yet again.

"Is she going to be all right?" Rodger questions.

Maggie shrugs, "I assume you are asking if she will regain her memory?" Her eyebrows lift.

His lips tighten.

"I can't say. The memory loss is not all that concerning when we remember what all we know she has been through and the multitude of trials she might have experienced. Your next question, will her memory return?" Rodger nods. "Well, I can't tell you; it might and it might not. One thing we do know, she speaks English. So what is your next step?"

"She," he points at Naydar, "Says this is Anna. Is that good enough?"

"It is for me," says Maggie, "It is for me." She pats his back and is heading toward the next patient when the door opens. Volunteers bring in four more mangled bodies. Maggie, Bobby, and everyone else snap into emergency mode. They exam, sort, and assign.

As one volunteer walks away, Rodger stops him. "Do you speak English?" The man pauses. Rodger repeats. "Do you," he says loudly, pointing at the man, "speak," he points at his mouth, "English?" The man thinks, then straightens, smiles, and points to another volunteer. Rodger waits till the indicated one turns to leave, then he approaches.

"Do you speak English?"

The man replies, "A bit, sir."

"What are you finding now, and are there other places you are taking them?" he indicates the injured in the room.

The intensity of the questions is duly noted. "Not many places, this one, two others. Most we find now dead. We take to old, er, planes..." the man imitates a landing aircraft.

"The airport?"

The man grins and points at Rodger. He offers a semi salute and leaves.

Rodger paces, both hands on his head. He checks his phone again, just in case. No signal. He approaches an interpreter and asks if there is someone who can go with him to the other medical facilities and the airport.

"Why, sir?"

"I need to make sure we have seen every possible survivor and victim to convince our authorities that the girl over there is who we think she is."

The interpreter walks to one of the volunteers. He explains the task. The man bobs a bow at Rodger, and motions toward the door.

"Naydar, don't leave her," commands Rodger as he turns to follow his guide.

"I will stay, Sab. I not leave Miss Anna."

Hours pass. Hours in which Rodger picks his way across tons of debris and rotting remains. He still sees groups of men digging with whatever they can find. Now and again they will see a search and rescue dog, which lets Rodger know that somewhere, someway, people are coming and attempting to aid in the rescue and clean up. The most heart-wrenching is women some young, some old, digging through what might have been their home or friends homes, searching, listening, crying. He passes every patient at every facility. No one fits Anna's age and general description. He shakes his head and they move on. Last stop after a good trudge is the airport, now home to the identifiable dead. Again Rodger passes down the rows of laid out bodies. Here there is a feeling of relief. Anna is not among these dead, not these.

It is dark by the time Rodger trudges back to check on the girl. He sighs, grimaces at the sleeping Naydar still in the same chair she occupied when he left hours ago.

Maggie wanders by, stops, "Well, what did you learn?"

"I learned that this girl is the only body that fits, only one close. Here she is. Right age, right look, speaks English. I learned there are so many injured that have been released to whatever family claimed them. Many, many dead. Lord, I hope I never see this many dead bodies in one day again. There is not much of a list as to who they were. The piles are being prepared for burning," Rodger stumbles on the word. He sags and leans against the wall, then regains his composure. "It seems so wrong. Piles of bodies about to be burned."

"Did you see the swarms of insects? As bad as it feels, it is best for these who survived. What would it be like to survive the storm only to die of a plague caused by trying to I.D. each body? If this were New York, and there were no cooling, no electricity, could you do any better?"

"Lord, I hope so. How is she?" He stares at the body on the bed.

"Fine, healing. She woke up once more, still has no memory, but each time she is more assured, mainly by Naydar. Those girls seem to have bonded."

"Yeah, I believe, if we prove she is Annalisel, I will have to get Naydar a visa for her new job."

Maggie examines the eyes in front of her. "Go home, get some sleep. Tomorrow will be a better fit if you are fit."

"How do you do this, Maggie?"

She shrugs and waves him toward the door. He walks the quiet way to the west, his path lit by torches of those who refuse to give up or rest.

Chapter 9

The clang of heavy metal wakes Rodger. He makes his way to the deck to see a strange looking ship out in the water offloading what appears to be earth-moving equipment. He calls for binoculars as the steward brings up his morning coffee. The man drops a bow and heads back toward the galley. Rodger sips and wonders at the ridiculous difference. Here he is on a luxurious yacht, sipping well brewed coffee, contemplating what he would like for breakfast, while twenty yards away lies a city in ruins with death and diseases rampant.

He hasn't heard from Amur and that concerns him. Each day Rodger goes to the clinic at least twice to check on Anna. Maggie still resists his attempts to get Anna out of the country. She seems to feel that travel over land would not be in Anna's best interest. He wants the girl out of here and safe, but perhaps, in a few days, the airport will be functional and flying her to the United States a better option.

He tries his cell phone, his first order of business each day. Lo and behold, he has a signal this morning. He watched workers climbing up on the only tower he could see yesterday, well good for them. His work, conducted on the radio via patched messages, is difficult, but today, he will be able to call in.

His binoculars arrive along with the announcement of breakfast. Rodger asks the man to bring it up on deck so he can view the on going work as well as keep an eye on the ship. When breakfast arrives, he thanks his crewman and waves him away. Most of the crew sneak off the boat each day to help with the work of re-establishing something resembling order amongst the ruins. Rodger knows this, but they don't know he is aware. Food reserves are getting low and soon there will have to be a run to Jakarta for the boat. He sighs. Too many details. He uses his phone to contact New York. It is still night there, but he leaves a message about two ongoing projects for his secretary and asks her to have James call him when he arrives at the office. Rodger is determined to green light what ever paperwork is necessary to bring Naydar to the states with Anna. Somehow, he feels she is a big part of the healing process. He then tries to call Phil, since he has a working phone. No answer. He finishes his meal, returns to his cabin to dress for the day, tells the captain to be prepared to do a food and medicine run tomorrow, and then heads toward the clinic.

Each day the view on his walk is different. He can tell conditions are improving, but it is so little and so slow. He shakes his head in frustration at the thought of all the logistical problems. Rodger remembers back to the Katrina debacle. It seemed so easy, bring in materials from neighboring states, only there were no roads, ports, airstrips available. Same song, another verse. There has to be a better way. He thinks of the clinic established in a forsaken house because it is all that is available.

Naydar is, as always, beside Anna's bed. The two of them are talking as he approaches.

"When did I come here?" He hears Anna whisper. "Where is here?"

It is good to hear her talking. She is still very weak, a bout with a respiratory problem hasn't helped. Naydar is patience personified. She never reminds Anna that she asked this question yesterday. She seems to instinctively know Anna needs to talk and she doesn't remember anything to talk about.

"You come to the island two weeks yesterday. You and mother and father. I am the maid where you stayed. Oh, Miss Anna, you have good time. Mem Benson, tell your dad, you not little girl, but a grown lady. I miss them."

"I wish I could remember. I try so hard, nothing,"

"Maybe better you not try so hard?" suggests Naydar. Anna grimaces, then she sees Rodger approaching.

"Hi," she says. "Is there any news?" No one has yet told her about her folks. They are waiting until she is stronger. Rodger suspects that she knows, but how, he doesn't know and he isn't about to bring that subject up.

"Well, I have news," he says. "My phone is functional. Anyone you girls would care to call?"

Anna leans forward, "You have bars?" She frowns, "Why did I say that? What are bars?"

Naydar drops her head, "No, sir. I have no one to call." Rodger wonders for the hundredth time about Naydar's family, what does she know and will she ever tell someone? He is pretty sure the officials will require family information for a visa. He scouts up Evelyn and asks her to see if she can get information from the maid and also to put any and all information they have on Naydar in a folder for him. She agrees.

Rodger returns to the two girls. He tells them what he saw on his way there. Naydar is interested; Anna is concerned. Something is nagging at her, but either she can't or won't put it into words, leaving open a lot of lines for speculation. "Naydar, I think Evelyn needs your help," says Rodger.

She nods and makes her way through to crowded room toward where a small desk sets. This is the "office" for this place. Soon Evelyn has the girl in deep conversation.

"So, are you anxious to get away from here to someplace nicer?" Rodger asks.

"I guess," answers Anna. "Where would someplace nicer be?"

"I am thinking New York. There will be better doctors, cleaner sheets, and well, you know."

Anna smiles, "I wish I did. I can't believe there are better doctors than Dr. Maggie. Maybe I could just stay here?"

Rodger's eyes fly open, he fights to calm himself before answering, "Maybe, but then, there are so many here who need that bed, we could take you to a more established place. I think you would like it."

"Do you like helping other people?" Anna asks.

He is stunned by the question and ponders how to frame an answer when Maggie relieves him of the necessity. "Sorry to break up your visit, but I have to examine my girl here, and then its meds time"

"Okay," breathes Rodger. "Could I have a brief word first?" He steps off to the side, as Maggie follows. "What if she doesn't regain her memory? How am I going to get her home?"

"Well, I'd say that is your problem, but if you're asking advice, I'd recommend that you talk to her about home instead of her *going* home. Make her see home in her head. Give her a reason to want to view it in person. Just saying." She taps her head, grins, and moves on. Perpetual motion, that is Maggie.

Rodger stays with Anna, joking with her about this big house with lots of staff members, and a little girl who hid in it, causing all the staffers to ransack the house to find her. "They finally found her asleep in the bathtub on the third floor," laughs Rodger. Anna giggles in response. When Naydar returns, Rodger excuses himself, stating he will visit later in the day, then he heads back to the boat and work.

The radio is sputtering as he boards. It is Phil returning his earlier call. Yes, they are back in Jakarta and no Amur didn't come with them. Rodger assigns Phil to make the first approach to the consulate in Jakarta about the Anna/Naydar extraction. "Get a list of everything we might need and for pete's sake remind them to be reasonable in their request for paperwork. They have to know what it is like here."

Phil's snappy, "Sure thing, boss," is gratifying.

Next, he reminds Phil that the boat will be in Jakarta tonight for supplies and he wants an update on the state of the Benkulu airport's progress. When do officials forecast it might be usable for air traffic.

Rodger spends the next five hours listening to reports and giving orders. His secretary brings him up to speed as best she can with an inconsistent signal. James reports on his findings concerning Anna's status and the house in upstate New York that Rodger hopes to have Anna in soon. The staff has been alerted, and Anna's governess/ nanny is setting up to receive her charge. Amur has already warned them to start the process. The information jangles a bit with Rodger, but he continues to check off his list. He adds a fax machine to the list of necessities that the boat will pick up and fires off a text to Phil to have it there. When he is finished with what he can get done, Rodger heads out to the clinic for the rest of the day and tonight. He is becoming adjusted to sleeping when and where he can and to helping with whatever he deems necessary at the clinic. Anything to preserve the company.

A pattern has developed. Rodger spends one hour in the morning at the clinic checking on the girls, then back to the boat and work, lunch, and more work. He returns to the clinic late in the afternoon. His conversations with Anna focus on the beautiful home awaiting her in New York. Anna listens. She asks questions, mostly about the house and grounds, rarely about people. For some reason, that strikes Rodger as odd. He questions Anna's lack of interest in the staff or people she might have known with Maggie. She shakes her head and again states this is not her area of expertise.

Evelyn provides Rodger with a folder of information on Naydar compiled from her interviews as well as those of the interpreters. It is a mighty slim folder. Naydar says her father was a fisherman, before the Boxing Day tsunami. He was killed trying to help pick someone out of the water. She and her mother came to Benkulu to work in the hotel after his death. Naydar doesn't remember any other family. Her mother worked in the office of the hotel until the day of this tsunami. That was the last time she remembers seeing her mother alive, but the hotel, office and all, is gone. Naydar worked as an individual hire for the wealthy families that flocked to the resort. She doesn't seem sure of the existence of any other family, she has no papers to back her story, and it seems a long shot at best to get her out.

Every two days or so, Rodger or someone of the crew goes to the airport to check on the progress. This is Germaine's day, and his report is that it will not be long before planes will be able to land at this airport. If they will be allowed to bring in privately owned planes is up to the officials in Jakarta. Phil has approached the U.S. consulate in Jakarta concerning the visas. James has acquired a copy of Anna's passport. Phil has an appointment with the Jakarta consulate to ask about a passport and visa for Naydar. It seems everything is advancing well, but Rodger can not shake his premonition. Something feels wrong. He watches Anna every day for any signs of her memory returning. She is Anna, she has to be.

Chapter 10

The path he takes to the clinic is surer, the ground firmer, the flotsam less annoying. Rodger is familiar with the way. He still watches the rescuers that are now more recoverers than rescuers because there are fewer and fewer new patients brought in. Each afternoon as he makes his way back to the clinic, he checks on anyone discovered that day. He sees no one fitting his requirements. Tonight he needs to work on Anna's memory and Naydar's possible extraction. He considers his arguments before arriving. Again he checks for additions as he walks through the building. To his surprise, there are three new bodies, live ones. None fit Anna's profile. He hunts up Maggie to discuss his requests. She isn't hard to find. He sees her leaning over a bed, one of the people just brought in, as usual, the most desperate one.

"Hi," he says. Maggie doesn't respond. "I need to talk with you, I have a couple of favors to ask."

"In case you haven't noticed, I am a bit busy." She never sees him. She is busy with the body on the bed.

"Well, might I talk with Bobby?"

"I am not his keeper," bites off Maggie. Rodger backs away from the area and goes in search of Bobby. He discovers him in the radio room deep in conversation with a third party.

"Look, I know what the problems are. I am here remember, but we need to start thinking about the next step. We need to be able to move these folks by at the least next week. If not, well I won't be responsible for their condition. It is hot, there are diseases everywhere. We need your help. No, the roads won't allow us safe overland travel as of yet. Yes, that does leave us with boats or planes. Why didn't I think of that? Look I am sorry, but it has been a very long day and … Yes, I will check back with you tomorrow."

"Bloody bugger. If he was born with any brains, they seeped out his pants years ago," Bobby mumbles as he wads up a list he has on the table in front of him. He tosses his head back and catches a glimpse of Rodger. "Oh, hi. You need something? We have tons and tons of nothing, but I might find you a blanket for the night."

Rodger grins at him. "I want to know what your procedures are for moving patients and closing down emergency centers such as this one. Think I've got part of my answer."

"Yeah, the nice, cool, air conditioned office division sees no reason for panic on my part. They figure we can wait till the roads clear up and then bring in some ambulance-type vehicles to take patients out more economically. Must keep our eye on the almighty, whatever the fuck this country's money is called. Hey man, I'm sorry, I'm..."

"Hot, tired, and weary of dealing with people who don't know and won't listen. About right?"

"On the head. Okay, what can I tell you and have you got a bleeding cigarette?"

"Tell me how things usually work, and why it might be a problem here," says Rodger as he fumbles in his jacket for a pack of smokes he has ordered just for Bobby.

Bobby lights a cigarette, leans back to take a drag, then begins to explain his world. "We are a triage unit. We fly in to the critical areas, set up an emergency room so to speak, and treat those we can, document everyone treated or untreatable, then make them ready for removal to a more secure advance medical facility. In most cases those are miles away instead of hundreds of miles away with no way to get there. Most of those we have here are broken bodies, like your friend, bouncing them around on those things referred to as roads right now would be painful, harmful and stupid, but it wouldn't cost much. Most of the time we inject antibiotics into the patients as a precautionary measure, here we used up all we brought with us as a necessity and, had you not brought extra supplies, I don't know what we would do. It was supposed, even when we discovered how extensive the damage was, that the airport would be functional by now to bring in supplies and to remove those patients that are removable."

"Removable?"

Bobby sighs, "Yeah, there are many here, that will die here. There is no point in removing them. We are basically keeping them comfortable, and trying to reunite them with any family. This wave plus the storm has separated many that are struggling to find each other while they try to find shelter and food. Each day is nothing more than a massive search for a large part of the population. Part of the day is spent searching for friends or family, the rest for enough food to survive till tomorrow and the cycle begins again. We have no idea of the identity or even nationality of many, as this area is such a large tourist area. We can assume the blue eyed blonds aren't from here, but even that is an assumption considering the business community. If they have no paper, can't talk, we are spinning wheels."

"So, when the airport is cleared? What then?"

"Then those who can be helped will be flown to an admitting hospital and the rest..." Bobby looks down at his hands and shrugs.

Rodger is floored. The young man he has considered callous, hard, unmoving, is not. His façade slips, his hands shake as he fights to regain control.

"Okay, here is what I know," says Rodger. "Phil says the airport will be available for traffic in about four days. The rescue operation is winding down to only recovery, so there is more personnel to devote to clearing and building. The world relief agencies are getting themselves organized. To put it in best of terms, help is on the way. Hang in!" Rodger reaches out and awkwardly taps the tensed shoulder.

Bobby tries a smile. He holds out his hand and wiggles two fingers to beckon another cigarette. Rodger hands him the pack.

"Thanks man, you know, you're not half as bad as I thought," Bobby's face pulls into a weary grin which resembles a grimace.

"Do you think there is any way Maggie would let me take Evelyn away from here for a couple of days?"

Now the expression slides toward suspicion. "Why?"

"I need to get Naydar through the vetting process to get a visa. Sorry to say, I'm not sure she trusts me all that much, and with Phil, she would be even more suspicious. I think we would have better results if she had Evelyn walking her around to the various agencies."

Bobby rakes his hand through the shaggy hair that has not seen scissors for the duration. "Let me ask her. I'll try to approach when she is more rested. Today isn't a good time."

"Yeah, I figured that one out. What's up her skirt?"

"Another one brought in by boat, from a place where the water is receding. She seems to think this one and your Anna might know about each other, but this one is in no shape to talk either. Yet."

"Another girl?" Rodgers feels the surge of blood pulse through his veins.

"Nope, a man. Seems about the same age. Might be interesting."

"Might. I'll take that blanket now. Sent the boat for more supplies."

Bobby throws him a cover, then smiles, "For that and another pack, I'll let you sleep in the radio room."

"Deal."

Rodger waves, and heads toward Anna. There he sits and visits. They discuss Anna's parents, her home in New York and her school in Switzerland. At dusk, Maggie makes her final rounds. She talks to Anna inquiring about her day, listening to each response. Rodger notices the lines around her mouth and eyes. She appears older than when they arrived a scant two weeks ago. His sudden revelation is that she is. So is he, and anyone else who has lived this mess. Anna, on the other hand, perks up at the sight of Maggie. She sits up taller in the bed to answer Maggie. She giggles as they talk about something that happened earlier. They both laugh about some mishap concerning Evelyn's skirt as Naydar looks from one to the other in total confusion.

Naydar turns toward Rodger. "What is funny?" she asks as she wrinkles up her nose. "Miss Evelyn is sweet lady. Why they laughing?"

Rodger shakes his head. He never understood female shenanigans even back in his boyhood amongst his sister's friends, and he doesn't now. But it was good to see smiles and hear laughter in this place so heavy with hurting and death.

Evelyn joins the group, pokes her finger first at Anna, then at Maggie, "Stop it, stop it I tell you. I will not be made the butt of your funnies. Naydar, are they telling tales again?"

Naydar nods and points at them both. "Silly, they be silly."

"Guilty as charged," Maggie chimes in. Then she walks away toward another bed, another patient, another burden to lift.

Evelyn indicates to Rodger that she needs him to step aside. The ever helpful Naydar pats Anna's bed, straightens her pillow and begins a new conversation.

"I found some new information on the girl," Evelyn explains. "I don't know if it will be useful, but she says she traveled to the Philippines with her mother last year visiting one of her mother's friends and searching for a job, something about a cruise line? Anyway, if that is true, there should be a passport or visa documentation at the consulate office."

Rodger thanks her and walks outside. He finds it interesting how beautiful the sky is here, how intense the stars. He doesn't remember paying much attention to them in New York. The bright lights there are so much different from here. Everything is. There is nothing further he can accomplish inside tonight. All his work begins now on the phone with his New York office. The merger that has eaten up months of his life has been set aside until things are settled. There has to be a clear title, an owner of the company, before any deals can be consummated. Rodger talks with his secretary about upcoming details. They devise a plan of action or inaction to handle the flow of information or lack thereof. Frustrated, he makes his next call to James. Here the news is more upbeat. Amur is on his way to Jakarta with the copy of Anna's passport. Rodger spends the next hour in consultation with two of the members of his management team about how to allay the fears of their potential merger partners. They develop a strategy for advancing once they get Anna's identity settled and the will through probate.

This conversation has Rodger calling James again to set in motion the probate and a guardianship agreement with him established as Anna's legal guardian until she is of age and declared fit. James agrees. Work stalls and Rodger sets out on his late night/early morning walk. Never one to need too much sleep, Rodger is bushed and proceeds to sack out on the floor of Bobby's radio room. To his surprise the morning light coming through the window wakes him to a new day. Bobby appears with a cup of coffee which he hands to Rodger while he tells him the good news for this morning. He has consulted with Maggie and she is letting Evelyn take Naydar to Jakarta. But Rodger is still leery of pushing the point without talking to Maggie. He approaches her in the back area where the staff is having breakfast.

She looks up at him and smiles. She must have slept well also. She indicates a seat next to her and pushes the platter of dried fruits toward him. Rodger shakes his head, "Thanks, but I'm good," he says. "I hear Bobby talked with you about my proposal. You sure you can get along without her? "

"I can *if* you do the interviewing and documentation work for however long she is gone."

Rodger taps his coffee cup to hers and agrees.

Chapter 11

The Indonesian day has barely begun when the crew from the yacht appears. Again they have food and some medications for the clinic. This is routine now, and they are taking boxes to the radio/storage area before Rodger is even on the scene. When he catches up with them he has Evelyn in tow, bags and all. They are seeking Naydar. For the first time since she was brought here, she isn't at Anna's side. They find her outside the clinic involved in morning prayers. She is told about her journey and its importance. "I am going to go to America with Miss Anna?" she asks, her face breaking into a smile that lights up the whole group. "Are you sure?"

"I will not promise," replies Rodger, "But that is what we want, and we need you to go with Miss Evelyn to get the necessary papers. Will you do that?"

"Yes, oh yes." She rushes to Anna's bedside, hurries through her explanation of her upcoming absence, then, snatching her few belongings, heads to Evelyn and the crew. Rodger has given his orders to them as to their meeting Phil at the dock with the girls and heading back as soon as possible. He likes his good guy role, but not to the point of sleeping on a cement floor indefinitely. He wishes them good seas and God speed then walks back to the radio room to inform Phil of his assignment.

Evelyn had suggested before she left that he needed to read the notes she made before talking with any of the patients. "Sure," he agreed, "I can see the need for that. You have to be sure they are telling the proper story and not trying to defraud insurance."

Evelyn sighed. "Naw, unlike your country, medical care here is free for all, even you, but we do need to know how lucid they are and if they remember new or differing facts, something that might help us to reunite them with family or friends."

Now he sits with Evelyn's notebook in hand to introduce himself to his new position. He tries to put faces with the names and stories on the pages before him. He is lost. He has been here every day, but only concerned with Anna and her care. He knows nothing about the others. He checks her notes.

The descriptions leave him frustrated. They contain only an approximate age, height, weight and an accurate gender. However, even in his short stay among the wounded, he realizes the futility of listing features that are torn, discolored, and that seemingly change with each day that passes. Beyond this meager information, there is nothing to help him determine the subject of the notation. He reads through a few, then an idea strikes. He rises and strolls from bed to bed looking at faces, checking charts, and adding bed numbers to the name in the notebook. Using his phone, he takes pictures of each patient with their number. Then he retreats to the storage room to study the information, planning to compile folders for elaborate records for each person. Problem is, there isn't any paper.

This should be his comfort zone. His strong suit is consolidating and analyzing information. He needs to gather the information that is available and put it into some form he can work with. Aboard his ship there is paper, a printer, and a recording devise. Lacking these materials, he reads through Evelyn's notes and sorts them by their account of how many are together with them when the wave approaches. He gazes again through the encounters, then re-sorts them by where they are when they become aware of the danger.

Again he reads the reports. He lays several to one side. Damn he needs his tools. Slowly he lays four out on the table side by side. He grimaces as he wonders if Evelyn will have a fit when she sees her notebook pages torn out. He checks the four he has out. Two of the accounts "see" the same scene at the beginning, the chaos that emerges divides the accounting souls. The place of rescue for each is within shouting distance of the other. Rodger clips the two together.

He examines the remaining two. Again the beginning view is identical, but one runs toward a street the other falters and slams into a structure. This is a possible, but not as strong as the first pair.

He continues to read, and review, focusing on the stated position when the event began. There are notes that do not contain much beyond a description. Rodger assumes these were victims too injured to be interviewed. He flips through once more and attaches a third paper to the second pair.

Rodger is excited about his potential discovery. He wants to share. He heads to "check" on Anna. She is sleeping. He pops his fingers. He is going to need an interpreter. He searches the area, but there are none in sight. The men who serve the facility as interpreters spend much of their time in actual rescue operations and have no set schedule. He finds this frustrating and makes a mental note to take it up with Maggie. Rodger feels like a kid who just learned to kick the football. He wants, nay needs, to tell or show somebody. Everyone here is busy.

As he awaits a time to discuss his findings, he sets out to discover what that big ship has managed to accomplish. He stays close by. In theory, he can see both the waterfront and the entrance to the clinic. He watches as a bulldozer is lifted over the side of the ship by crane and lowered to the ground. It promptly sinks down to above the wheels. All attempts to lift it back to the ship are laughable, causing a dangerous tilt to the ship. After several tries, the bulldozer is disconnected and abandoned. One of the workers then heads toward the clinic. Rodger recognizes him as one of the three interpreters. He waves and follows the man inside. They head to the back area to get a cup of coffee and to discuss this afternoon's new assignment. The interpreter whose name is Kasim, suggests they ask Maggie how to unite the groups that Rodger has identified. That requires them searching Maggie out – not always an easy task – and laying out their request. Maggie listens and looks at the patients that Rodger wants to move. She decides which of the group would be least affected by moving. "Damn, I wish we had a wheelchair."

"Yeah," mutters Rodger, "and I wish I had a steak, but what is the best alternative, pick up a mattress?"

Kasim's dark eyes narrow. He taps his tilted head. His eyes light up. "Wheelbarrow. We have wheelbarrows. I will get one from the center site."

"Are they needed there?" asked Maggie.

"Yes, but not so much that we cannot bring one here for a while." He is forward in his chair and seems halfway out the door. Maggie

The Wave Effect 61

nods her approval and he is gone. "Call me before you attempt to move anyone," She admonishes Rodger.

He acknowledges her, but she is gone before he is up. Rodger checks his watch and goes back to rereading notes and waits, something that is not in his comfort zone. This is the most difficult part of Rodger's participation; he is not used to waiting.

Two hours later, Kasim and the other two interpreters approach the building with a wheelbarrow. Rodger has talked with Phil, the girls are delivered and they have an appointment at nine in the morning with the passport office and an appointment with US ambassador to talk visa.

Kasim grins, indicates his two companions and says, "We found one. Took us a while to get it down."

"Down?"

"Yes," says the second man, "It was in a tree. Silly wave."

Rodger chuckles as he leads the way to a young boy about ten to twelve years of age. He looks to be an Indonesian with dark wavy hair and dark eyes. His slender torso is covered with bruises. One eye is almost swollen shut while the other is black. One arm is in a sling, both legs are bandaged, and his torso has a tight wrap. Rodger is aghast that this is the one Maggie has chosen to move. The men move to either side of the boy. Maggie explains that they are going to take him around to another building. She does not say why.

Four sets of hands move toward the boy's body. He bites his lip in anticipation. All eyes are on the child's face as they scoop him up in their arms and lay him in the wheelbarrow which has been cushioned with every available blanket. They lower him tenderly to the center of the makeshift cushion. He groans but does not cry out. Maggie wipes the sweat from her upper lip. She looks at the child. He smiles up at her, causing grins and relief all around.

Maggie leads the way. Rodger is feeling a bit left out as the last of the interpreters pushes the boy though two rooms into a long room packed side to side with grown men. He is wheeled to the next to last bed on the north side. There a man lies, his hand over his face, his eyes closed, both legs perched on a table placed beneath a sheet on the bed. The boy looks at the man. Words that Rodger cannot begin to understand rip from the youngster's mouth. He tries without success to climb out of the wheelbarrow, almost turning it over. Two of the helpers grasp it while the third and Rodger grab the boy. The man opens his eyes. He sees the group in front of him. Rodger doesn't need an interpreter. He is calling the name of his child, or his nephew, or his kin. Rodger bets on child. Tears stream down the faces of the man and the boy. Soon everyone within earshot is crying.

Maggie explains to the interpreters that she is okay with leaving the boy there for a short while, but one of them must stay and after a short visit, Kasim and Rodger need to return to listen to the pair tell their story. She sets a one hour limit for the boy to be out of bed. As they walk away, Rodger suggests to Maggie that while the pair talk, they could move the boy's bed next to the man's. "I'll think about it" is the only answer he receives.

He returns to his "desk" at the back of Anna's room. From here he can review the notes Evelyn's took while keeping his eyes on Anna. What annoys him is why are there no names? It has to be much easier if they tag every patient by first and last name. He gets those who are unable to talk but the others? Sloppy work, just sloppy. He shakes his head as he rereads the story of the boy and his father. Why did the father not report he had a son? He feels Evelyn would have caught that.

With hands that shake, he leafs through the notes on this boy and his father. The boy reported searching for marine life on the beach with his father in front of the Benkulu resort hotel when the wave hit. He could see his mother motioning for them to return. Dad turns, grabs his arm and starts running toward the hotel. The wave hits them, tears him from his father He tumbles through the wave to the top, takes a breath, sees a log floating nearby, grabs it and holds on. A cat is on the log with the boy. He glimpses his father, watches as his father goes under the wave. He didn't see father again. The log is headed out away from the shore with him and his feline companion clinging in desperation. They are spotted and pulled out by a fishing crew after what seemed hours. The fishermen brought him to the clinic three days ago. There is only a scribbled Ka at the end. No last name that Rodger can see.

The Wave Effect 63

The father's story is identical until the separation. The father tells of diving under searching for his son. He grabs the arm of his boy and then is slammed against a crumbling building. He doesn't remember much after the hit except hanging on to his son's arm with one hand and grasping at a column of some sort with the other. He remembers the water going over his head several times but always retreating enough for him to breath. His eyes are struck by debris and he is confused. His strength is giving way when a boat approaches. He calls out and the boat heads his way. A swell raises the boat and it slams his legs against the column. He hands his son up to the boat with his last ounce of strength, two rescuers come into the water to save him only to tell him his son is dead. He doesn't give Evelyn a name; he doesn't speak to anyone. He is sedated.

How impossible is it to identify kith and kin in this confusing environment, wonders Rodger. How many are waiting to have their stories linked? He wishes for the nth time his office computer was available with all its connections, but it isn't and this must be done one fact at a time. He looks back toward the father's bed. Kasim motions for him to come. It is time to interview the pair. The lad says his name is Jokor Kalem. Father's name is Ali. His family including mother and two sisters were in Benkulu on a holiday. On the day of the tsunami, father and son are walking on the beach. Ali nods as he listens to Jokor's story. They spy mom and sisters on the balcony of the hotel waving frantically at them.

Father interrupts to pick up the narrative. He turns to see the wave, grabs his son and starts running. Jokor is faltering. The wave strikes them from behind, they tumble under the water. He loses control of Jokor's arm. He surfaces but does not see Jokor.

Jolar speaks up, "But I saw you, you were between me and the hotel. I saw you go back under, then I grabbed the log, I didn't see you come up."

Father reaches out his hand and takes the boys small arm. "I swam under water looking for you," Ali says. "I spotted a boy. I thought he was you, I grabbed him and swam toward this brick column that was out of the water. We slammed into the column. I try to turn Jokor, I mean the boy, but he hits it too. I saw a metal bar sticking out, I grabbed it and held on until a boat comes. My legs are useless, I hand up my son, but they tell me he is dead. They pull me into the boat and bring me here. I hurt but I don't care. Everything I care about is missing or dead."

Rodger pauses to make sure the two are finished, then he asks through Kasim, "Tell me exactly who you saw around you on the beach. Did you now any of them by name?"

The two look at each other and begin to talk. Kasim interrupts and Rodger waits. They come up with three names that they are sure of, four names that they aren't confident about, and descriptions of a half dozen more people from the beach. Rodger then draws their attention to the hotel. Again, the two describe people they saw around the entrance, on balconies, and on the street in front. With father prompting son and son prompting father, they describe about thirty more people. Maggie walks up and calls a halt to the interrogation for today. Father and son speak their goodbyes. Kasim pushes Jokor back to his area. As they pass a bed, he points to the man on the bed blurting out a phrase. The man on the bed glances at Jokor and speaks. This happens again in Jokor's room. The occupant in the bed is a youngster, but the reaction is much the same.

When their young patient is safely lifted back into place, Maggie checks him out and delivers his meds. The three retreat to Rodger's "desk".

"Okay, what was that all about?" he asks Kasim

"The boy recognized the two as being on the beach, one he named."

Rodger looks at Maggie, "You expected this, didn't you?"

She shrugs, "Memory is a funny thing. It sometimes requires a prompt. Kasim, when you have time to talk to Ali again, see if he remembers anything about the rescuers."

"Why?"

"The memory is a funny thing, sometimes it needs a prompt," Maggie repeats. "They are going to remember too."

"They are busy," Rodger reminds her.

"Yes, but at times they need to stop and rest. What better place to rest than here where they can see what they have accomplished rather than think of the task ahead."

Kasim nods agreement before heading back to who knows where.

Chapter 12

As he accepts responsibility for writing them down, Rodger immerses himself in the stories. Horror after horror seeps from the pages into his brain. He has been here, it is not like he just arrived, but it seems as if he knows nothing of what happened. That girl whose face is covered with bandages, she slid down a building trying to grasp something, anything to hold on to. Her face was left as part of the façade. It is tightly wrapped to squeeze what remains preventing bleeding. So no sound is heard except for the frequent moan that he tries to block from his hearing. Broken bodies now fill his consciousness as people, rather than bed numbers. The last name exemption becomes obvious as he realizes how few can form cohesive language. Those who can have a scribble of letters near their name. Then there is a local custom concerning the naming of names. Rodger doesn't understand, but this is their land and that he is beginning to understand.

Kasim and his fellow rescue workers are spending more time at the clinic as fewer souls are available for rescue. The Army has arrived to help with the retrieval of bodies, the identification of those that can be identified, the removal of said bodies, as well as the ever increasing debris that still floats up each day. The bodies building up at the airport are being disposed of after the right hands are removed. There is a greater emphasis on identifying those that are not local. This seems so unfair to him, even as he reminds himself that he is a visitor and is hoping to claim a visitor.

Evelyn returns and claims her desk with a surprise. She has DNA that Amur brought to expedite the delivery of Anna to their custody. The airport at Benkulu is to open for planes tomorrow and Benson Enterprises now has three in Jakarta. The one which will be here tomorrow will be his personal jet prepared to take him, Anna, and hopefully Naydar to the states. Phil is turning that one over to Dave who will serve as pilot while he continues coordinating business interests through Jakarta.

Plans are for there to be a visa waiting for Naydar when the plane returns there, then this group can head to New York. If Naydar has to wait, Amur will stay with a second company jet to bring her when she clears. The third bigger plane will land tomorrow to carry as many of the patients who can be moved to Jakarta or even Darwin. Rodger foresees Maggie, Bobby, and Evelyn on that plane. Of course, he doesn't discuss his plans with the group.

Bobby approaches with his usual half smile. "DNA is a perfect match. Interesting that they didn't check her fingers. Is that because of the broken bones or just too much red tape?"

"I don't know," frowns Rodger. "Amur took care of the identification. Maybe. How many of her fingers are broken?"

"Three"

"Well, I guess that's your answer." He starts to walk away; Bobby catches his arm.

"How well do you know this Amur?"

"Not well, he and Carl worked together."

Bobby shrugs, rolls his eyes, and saunters back to the radio room. Rodger follows him with his eyes and frowns. He whips out his phone and sends off a text to James asking for more information on Amur and his connection to the company. Then he heads toward Anna's bed finding Naydar beside her as usual. The girls are laughing. Anna reaches up to smooth her hair away from her forehead, a grimace crosses her face and her eyes close, but no sound is emitted.

He is New York ready. There he understands the language, the customs, the motives. He is tired of confusion; he is ready for control. Whatever must be done to get this whole problem back to home base, Rodger is for doing. He smiles and says his goodbye to the girls and heads for the boat. That is something else he is tired of. This boat that was so welcome only days ago, seems now cramped. It is time for the adventure to end, and the real world, real job, real life to begin. At the boat there is a surprise waiting. Maggie sits in the bow with a glass in hand. Along with her are Bobby and Evelyn. Warily, he approaches the trio. "Is there a party I don't know about?"

"Yep," answers Maggie. "We came to say farewell. We even ordered up some of your booze to celebrate. To be honest, I wasn't in favor of you in the beginning," starts Maggie, her statement eliciting hoots from Bobby and Evelyn and even a tiny grin from Rodger.

"I would never have known," he cracks.

Maggie lifts her first finger up to beckon silence. "No, I thought you would be a liability to all we were sent to do. But here I stand, hat, well figurative hat, in hand, apology on lips ready to admit to all that I was wrong."

"Take this down, Bobby," says Evelyn. "This is definitely a first."

Bobby grins salutes with his drink as he claps Rodger on the shoulder. "Here here. Before we order a second round, would you like to catch up?"

The orderly offers Rodger a tray with his favorite cocktail. Rodger shakes it off and orders Champagne for everyone. The others look at him in amazement, "What?" mocks Maggie, "You have had champagne here all this time and we never knew?"

"Had it brought in last shipment," he smiles, "In anticipation of this very moment."

"Can't get ahead of you no matter what," grins Maggie. The party sits down and the reminiscing begins. Each has a story or insight to contribute. They are mellow, relaxed and comfortable with each other. Rodger remembers that first meeting and how different his perception. When he admits he thought Bobby was the doctor, Maggie laughs and Bobby spits champagne. Things begin to settle down as the conversation turns to the now and the future. "Why don't you trust Amur?" Rodger asks of Bobby.

Bobby swirls the wine in his glass, scans Rodger's face, and responds, "I'm not keen on him."

"Hey, you weren't keen on me either, as I recall."

"Yeah, but we knew where you were coming from. You weren't hiding what you wanted or why. Amur, I pick up different vibes. His eyes don't agree with his words." Bobby grins and lifts the glass, "Silly thing went and got empty on me. "Garcon, more bubbly."

The mood swings back, and the party continues. Rodger tells them of the plane that will be at their disposal beginning tomorrow. Maggie frowns, which confuses Rodger. "We belong to an international organization. We go when, where, and *how*, they say. Thought you understood that."

"Well, since our plane brought you here, I guess I thought we would finish it out and see you home again. The plane is equipped to carry patients, and Phil is charged with taking you wherever you wish to go. Our way of saying thank you for all you have done here and elsewhere."

Mollified, Maggie settles down and thanks Rodger for his concern.

"Where will you be going?" he asks.

"It is a fluid situation at the moment. Jakarta is rather full, they will let us know before we begin to load."

"Then what? I mean after you find hospitals to take these, what is next? Do you head back to Australia?"

"Perhaps. Until the next disaster, natural or manmade," Evelyn states.

Again the chatter turns to the past and what they have done here and in other situations. It is fascinating to Rodger to contemplate all their adventures. He isn't sure he is prepared to leave this group behind. Ideas for them in America, close to him, begin to sprout in his brain. He is aware of an internal tug. The party is interrupted when a call comes in to Maggie's phone. Someone has a need and they are up and gone.

The new day produces its own problems. After he makes his usual trek to Anna's bedside, where he chats with her and the ever present Naydar, he checks in on Jokor and his father. The two are spending more time together as they heal. There is no mention of the mother or two sisters. He wanders past the girl with the bandaged face, still mummified. It is as if the place has become a real hospital, not the warehouse it was or will be again. Rodger keeps his phone near and the buzzer on as he awaits the arrival of Dave and the first of the planes. Officials come by bringing Maggie the paperwork on Anna. They have accepted the DNA results. As Maggie congratulates Rodger, she states, "They are as thrilled as you are. One less for them to deal with. I'll be shocked if Naydar's request is denied. They are hoping for as many placements as they can find."

"Possibly, but it is the USA that will have the last say on Naydar."

"Ech, they won't be too strict since she has a job, a place to stay and someone to care for her. It will go through. Those girls are cute together."

"Maggie, do you think Anna will ever regain her memory?"

"As a physician I have to admit I don't know. As Maggie, I think so. What it will take to jog her out of her defenses and into her past, I can't say."

"Will she remember it all? The tsunami, her parent's deaths?"

Maggie just shrugs, blows him a kiss and hurries down the hall. Rodger shrugs in return trying to remember if he has ever seen her not in a hurry.

In walks Dave, waving papers in his hands. Naydar is cleared, Anna is cleared, the plane will be ready to take off in three hours. Everyone hikes into high gear. Within an hour Anna is ready to transport, Naydar has her possessions, Rodger's boat has sailed. Maggie and Evelyn hug goodbyes as Bobby approaches from the radio room. Rodger grasps each hand and thus this chapter ends as the next challenge begins.

Chapter 13

Jakarta is the first stop on the way back to normal. Here there is evidence of the storm, but not the tsunami. Here there is traffic, noises that are familiar and common to any city. Here the plane checks in, and fuels for the trip to New York. A medical team boards briefly to check on Anna's condition before deplaning, leaving behind a nurse in scrubs with a stethoscope around her neck. Yes, *her*. Dave is at the controls with a co-pilot, unknown to him, assisting. In mere moments they are once again in flight. Next stop, New York. It is night here and when they land, it will be night, one day will be gone, one curtain closed and Rodger, for one, is beyond ready. He settles into a seat. If this were a usual trip, he would be in the private room of the plane preparing to sleep the flight away or at his desk working. But Anna is in the bedroom with the nurse, Naydar is at the desk fiddling with some icons she brought with her, and he gets stuck in a passenger seat. Only a week ago this would have garnered his ire, but he is so relieved he cares not for the comfort of his private bed room. He is asleep within the hour.

The steward assigned to this trip offers food. Rodger picks at his as Naydar examines hers with great curiosity, Anna isn't awakened, and the nurse inhales hers as if she hasn't eaten in days. There are no other interruptions until the announcement of the landing. Startled, Rodger realizes he has not made arrangements to be met or transported. He is relieved when he sees a company car escorting an ambulance on the tarmac. At least someone is awake and thinking. That someone hops from the car as soon as the plane parks. When the door opens, James is at the door of the ambulance with two men in EMS uniforms. Rodger waves them aboard. Before anyone else is allowed to leave, Anna is checked out and turned over to the EMS officials. Naydar is upset when she is told that she cannot ride with Anna. Anna is also upset, confused, and bewildered. Rodger takes time and convinces them to let Naydar ride in the ambulance. Then he joins James in the car as the procession sets out.

It takes a while for Anna to be processed into the private hospital that James has chosen. He assures Rodger that the hospital is first rate with an excellent orthopedic department and a highly recommended psychology division. Anna will be in capable hands. Once the two girls are situated in the private suite allotted them, the men leave, promising to return. Anna's face twists in fear but she bravely nods goodbye. Rodger pats her shoulder, taps Naydar on the head, "Take care of our girl," he says.

"Yes sir, I will stay right here," she promises. He laughs. Where else would she go?

At the office, James pours drinks, then sets about catching him up on all pertinent information. The memorial service for the Bensons will be held a week from tomorrow with hopes that Anna will be able to attend. The business is reeling from the loss of the Bensons, however some areas are beginning to stabilize. There are documents on his desk in order of importance for Rodger to work on. He fingers the pile of papers, but his mind is tinkering with the Anna problem. "Talk to me about Amur," he asks James.

"Well, he worked mostly with Carl. There is nothing in his file to cause suspicion. He has no family listed except a sister who lives in Indonesia."

Rodger's head jerks up, "Where in Indonesia?"

"A smallish village in the mountains near Benkulu. Look, the name of the town is right there. I can't pronounce it." He points to the sheet in his hand.

Rodger grabs the document, probes it. Nothing draws his attention.

"What's the deal with Amur?"

"Nothing, I just wish I knew more about him. We've trusted him with a lot of information."

"What information?"

"Anna's birthplace, her school in Switzerland, the place upstate where she was raised, you know – personal stuff."

"He probably already knew that. I understood he and Carl were quite close."

Rodger shakes off his premonitions, picks up the paperwork from his desk as he heads toward the door. "Let the folks at the Benson estate know to prepare for Anna and Naydar. I want them there as soon as Anna is fit to be home. Meanwhile, I want someone from security outside her room."

"Why?" James is perplexed.

"I'm... I... Just do it." Rodger stops in the reception area long enough to let his secretary, Claire Dailey, know he will be at the hospital and what calls she is to put through to him. James is left standing glass in hand, mouth open, and no idea what has occurred.

Back at the hospital, he discusses Anna's prognosis with her doctor. There will be a surgery tomorrow to set bones. Not a big deal the Doctor assures him. Back in her room, the girls welcome him. They are both feeling somewhat abandoned. The atmosphere in the room improves. On the bed, Anna visibly relaxes as Naydar starts some silly story about what a nurse said when she delivered the last round of medication. Rodger settles into a desk in the room inspecting the papers he brought with him. He divides them into two stacks, one for tonight and one for the morning.

He is halfway through tonight's work when a soft tap on the door draws his attention. He cracks the door, observes the young man in a suit, and steps out in the hall. Behind him the room is quieter, the girl's chatter has slowed, they appear drowsy. The hospital is settling in for the night. The young man flashes identification at Rodger. This is the security that James acquired. He taps on the door to announce his entrance, then steps in with the young man. Everyone is introduced, then Rodger explains to the girls that the young man will remain outside unless they want anything. His job is to procure whatever they need.

"Are you leaving?" Anna's big eyes implore.

"I'll be back in the morning, you know, our regular routine." His smile reassures. "Meanwhile Dereck will be on the door, right Dereck?"

"Yes, sir, I mean yes, ma'am. I will be right outside. No problem." His stuttered response brings short, soft giggles.

The door is closed behind Rodger and he charges the youngster. "Anyone going in that room will have identification from the hospital, or it will be Mr. Stanton, or myself, understood."

"Yes, sir," now the young man is puzzled, but he accepts his assignment.

"If a doctor goes in, I want a name and a report when he leaves. I will be here in the morning." With that Rodger walks away toward the door, the city he loves, and the apartment he hasn't seen in a while. Once inside he breathes slowly, checking out the place that has been home for so long. Here there is nothing that is personal, all the photographs on the wall are places he has been or would like to go, the style is professionally perfect as is the reputation of the firm hired to decorate. He is home, but home feels less than homey. He shrugs and gathers his papers.

The night's work finished, Rodger relaxes in his chair and ponders his position. He is restless, yet he needs rest. He finds an old sleeping pill, is about to take it when his phone rings. When he see Phil's number, all thoughts of sleep flee and he is back in the saddle, running a twenty-four-hour company. Conversation over, he allows himself four hours of sleep before he greets a new day. He works at the hospital while Anna is in surgery then heads to his office awaiting a call to let him know she is awake. Back to the hospital he goes. The doctor's report is very optimistic, Anna's injuries, while substantial, were not exasperated by the delay in treatment. Oh to be young. The doctor has high praise for her emergency caretakers. As this day draws to a close, Rodger is already preparing for tomorrow.

This new day will set a pattern for the week ahead. Rodger arises, bathes, dresses, heads straight to the hospital were he takes his breakfast with the two girls who are virtual prisoners in the hospital suite, one by way of her injuries, the other by her unfamiliarity with her surroundings, the language, and New York dress. Naydar insists on wearing her head covering anytime she is outside. Then he goes to work at his office while a security person stays outside the door. He receives regular reports both from security and from the medical staff.

At the office he is ever the COO, dealing with whatever arises, watching the market both here and abroad. He finds himself thinking of Maggie and her medical team. The moment passes and he is back to the grind. At six, he returns to the hospital to relieve the day person and welcome night security. No problems have occurred, and James wonders out loud if the security is needed. Rodger eats supper with the girls and listens as they describe their day.

They watch television, play cards, talk and nap. At least Anna naps. Naydar is picking up more and more English and slang from the TV. Rodger is amused and relieved. She is going to be fine. Anna too is improving day by day. She is more secure, alert, and confident. She seldom asks about her parents or her life here. Until today.

Rodger arrives, sits down at the small table the three regularly gather around for their morning meal. Anna waits until he has begun to chew before asking, "Where did my family live?"

He almost chokes, which gives him a space to think. Did she use past tense? She knows. When? Who? How did she discover this truth? It wasn't that they had lied to her, the psychologist thought it would be better dealt with as things progressed. That was what her report said.

"You had... er, have a penthouse in Manhattan. It is a lovely place close to the park. Carl was forever talking about you playing in the park."

"My Father?"

"Yes"

"And my Mother, what was her name?"

"Maria. Do you remember them?"

"No, yes, I don't know." Her hands rise to her brow. "It's that sometimes... " She stops. "I didn't call her that." Statement of fact. Rodger has no idea what to say, and for once in his life he says nothing. Anna drops the train of thought and the breakfast resumes. Conversation focuses on last night's soccer game. He hadn't known there was a soccer game. He finishes and prepares to leave for the day.

"Naydar, could I see you?"

"No talking about me," Anna frowns. "What do you want to know?"

"Who told you about your parents?" He stands, waiting for an answer.

Anna's head dips, "Then it is true."

Naydar is distraught. "I told her they die. We saw something on TV about a service?"

Rodger processes the information then asks Naydar to join him outside. Anna isn't pleased but she doesn't protest.

"What did you tell her?"

"Only that her parents died in Benkulu, nothing else."

"Nothing about the tsunami or the storm or what happened to her,"

"No, sir. I couldn't. How does one explain a tsunami? And I don't rightly know what happened to her. Do you know, sir?"

"No, but anything you tell Anna the lady doctor needs to know. Okay?"

Naydar nods agreement, her face still full of worry.

"You are fine," he reassures her. "We all need to know what she is told so we can better determine her future, understood?"

Naydar drops her head. Rodger puts his finger under her chin, lifts her head and smiles at her. Then turning his head sideways, he glances into her worried eyes. "We're fine." He pats her head and winks at the employee on the door as he prepares to start his work day.

Chapter 14

Anna has been in the hospital four days. Her injuries are healing. Her hands are still bandaged, her ribs are wrapped, and the bruises on her head and torso are still visible, but the doctor is agreeable to a move to the penthouse. The psychiatrist hopes that in a familiar setting, Anna will begin the process of regaining her memory. They all hope that soon her past is part of the present. Ms. Dailey, Rodger's secretary. following the recommendations of Dr. Walker, Anna's psychiatrist, engages a nurse to stay at the apartment full time. She, along with the ever present Naydar and the housekeeper, will complete Anna's temporary family. The move is accomplished with little fanfare. Again the disconnect between the place where she is comfortable and her new position creates confusion. Anna is pale from the exertion, but otherwise no hiccups. Rodger is again grateful for the continuity Naydar's presence provides. She is Anna's anchor, the reassurance that all does not change.

They have three days until Carl and Maria's funeral service.The plans are to have a public service here, then take the bodies back to Utley, New York for a smaller private service and burial. Several decisions must be made. Should Anna attend both, one, or neither of the services, and then, will she resettle in Utley?

He always thought running a corporation was difficult, but he finds making decisions for another person increasingly time consuming. He falls behind, and he knows it. At least Phil has returned to help with logistics. A flight to prepare the Utley estate is a breeze for the cocky youngster compared to his last few assignments. Amur phones in but remains in Jakarta much to Rodger's relief. He isn't prepared to deal with his strong sense of dread. Again and again, he casts his mind back to Benkulu and his brief time with Amur. There is something that nags at his brain but refuses recognition. He dismisses this line of thought and puts in a call to the psychiatrist's office explaining his desire to have a brief conversation with Dr. Walker, then settles back into the work on his desk.

He is deep in the coils of reviving and revising the potential merger that fell apart while he was in Indonesia when the doctor returns his call. They discuss Anna and the upcoming services. Dr. Walker schedules a home visit for tomorrow morning, suggesting it might be best if Rodger is there.

He sighs and adds one more interruption to his agenda. The long day gets longer, but he still takes time to go to the penthouse for supper before returning to the office. When he finally makes it home he has six hours before he is to be up, dressed, and out the door.

Dr. Walker arrives on time. She accepts the offer of breakfast where the conversation flows freely over subjects that have no bearing on any therapy or anyone's future. Anna starts out wary, but relaxes when the subjects discussed are not her. Shortly, Dr. Walker and Anna retreat to her room where the doctor probes her attitudes and fears. After the session Rodger offers to see Dr. Walker to her cab. She tells him, in her opinion, Anna is capable of attending the services as long as the media can be kept at bay. It might even be the time jog that they are hoping for. He agrees, calls her cab, and is back in the office within the hour.

Three days of concentration on what Rodger refers to as his real job has its affect. He becomes more confidant, assured, and harder to startle.

James comes in frequently to discuss business other than Anna. He hasn't started the estate proceedings. They have time for that after the burial. He has recorded the death certificates for both of the Bensons and hopes Anna regains her memory before they get to the will. He draws up papers of guardianship so Rodger will continue to serve in that capacity until a thorough search for any possible relatives can be made.

The first rate team of lawyers from his office spend vast amounts of time pouring over all law pertaining to the transferring of estates to persons with memory lapse. Before they open that can of worms, they want every case researched. The best outcome is the regaining of her memory. Until then everyone concerned with Benson enterprises treads lightly and speaks in circles. So far, the market has given them a pass since the original downward spiral. Each day that passes with no more exasperating news brings a bit of an uptick.

Benkulu, Indonesia and the tsunami are old news. The market, business, oh hell, the world dotes on the new and what have you done for me lately. Doctor's International becomes another charity for consideration, and their team disappears into the mist of yesterday. The now, the necessary, the immediate absorbs every ounce of energy. And tomorrow? Well, it will have to wait, there is too much to slug through today.

Rodger makes one last call to Dr. Walker for reassurances both that Anna is ready and that the Doctor will be there. The funeral company arranges a side area for the family, closed off from the view of the general population. Security sets up to manage both the traffic and any situation that might reflect badly on either Carl and Maria or their company. The last thing Rodger needs is a protest the like of some he has seen at prominent funerals. Tomorrow then, maybe he, well, all of them can find a firm ground to build upon.

He completes his list and is about to head to the penthouse when Ms. Dailey buzzes. "What?"

She ignores the terse answer. "A Doctor Burrell is on the line. She says it is important."

Maggie? Now. What could she want? "Put her through."

"Hello Maggie. Are you all well?"

"Yes. Remember the young man that was brought in from the same area as Anna? We brought him with us to Darwin. He is much better and he has a story you need to hear."

"Can it wait? The Benson's funeral is tomorrow and there is still much that needs doing. If you give my secretary your phone number, I'll get back to you in a day or so."

"You should hear this as soon as possible. Is Anna okay?"

"Sure. She hasn't regained her memory but otherwise…" the line goes dead. A crack of thunder in the distance gives him the excuse he needs. Ms. Dailey is at her desk when he comes out hat in hand. "Please retrace that last call," he orders. "It is important and I will need to get back to her tomorrow or at least the day after."

She smiles, marks her note pad, and he makes his way to the elevator. He is halfway to the lobby when the office phone rings again. Ms. Dailey also has her jacket on, her briefcase packed and is headed toward the elevator. She looks at the phone, checks her watch and punches the down button. Tomorrow. She will deal with it tomorrow.

Chapter 15

He dreads this day. Carl was a friend as well as his boss for the past twenty-three years. He was the brash young man fresh out of college who knew business from the days of his lemonade stand through funding his college education by working in brokerage houses. He came to his interview with this rising star of energy technologies exuding all the confidence of someone who knows they belong. Carl was amused; his chief consultant was not. James Stanton saw an opinionated, egotistical, hothead. He was correct, but Carl hired the young man against Stanton's advice and a friendship and working partnership ensued.

The two argued as they bounced ideas off each other and pitched them off the solid dependable James. They partied together; they laughed together. When they fell in love - Rodger with Janet and Carl with Maria, James toook care of the legal issue. When Janet left Rodger for another man, Carl was there with a sympathetic ear, James with a divorce settlement. And when Carl's daughter was born prematurely, his friends ran the company freeing him to be with his family. But mainly they all worked together to build up this company, one from the legal department, one from the office in New York where he was comfortable amongst the bankers, lawyers, and brokers that swarm around any successful business, especially one that takes off and grows as fast this one, the other from the compartment of a jet taking him from country to country and site to site with Maria at his side until Annalisel is born. Then Maria goes often, but not always. Rodger could not have done it without Carl's capital and expertise, and Carl needed Rodger's business acumen. It was a perfect pairing except now Carl, the owner and head of the business is gone.

The limousine picks up Rodger then James, dropping them at the Cathedral before making its way to the penthouse. The two go inside and check all of the final arrangements. There are a few pictures of the family that show on a projector. The place reeks with sweet aroma from hundreds of flower arrangements that surround the biers waiting for the arrival of the two caskets. James looks about, checks some of the cards in the pile beside the flowers, walks to the front of the building and signs in.

Meanwhile Rodger is inhaling and remembering. The flowers for some reason have reproduced memories of *that smell*! Why is unfathomable. This is a pleasant odor, a cool quiet atmosphere, but his senses are dragging him back in time to that place, that heat, *that smell*. He is visibly upset, but James believes it to be his reaction to the death of his friend and gives him space. The caskets are delivered only minutes before the group from the penthouse arrive. The girls are somber, Anna in a plain black dress and a black head scarf that had originally belonged to her mother, and Naydar in a dark, flowing gown with a matching Indonesian head covering. Rodger wondered where she found that. They are here early to keep them from the growing crowd outside and to give Anna a bit of time with her parents. The funeral director hangs close in case anything is needed. Dr. Walker asks the question on everyone's mind, "Anna, would you like to see them?"

Anna's face is already the color of chalk, and frankly, Naydar's isn't far behind. "I think so," she whispers. The director approaches the caskets and lifts one. Anna gazes upon the dead face of her mother. Naydar steps to her side. The girls whisper. Then the second lid is raised. Again the process, first Anna and then Naydar. The rest of the gathered assembly make their way past the two coffins. The director asks Rodger if they would like the caskets to be open or shut during the ceremony. He looks at Anna and the doctor. Dr. Walker questions Anna. She shakes her head violently. The director retreats and closes the caskets. The two trembling girls are taken back to another area to calm before the crowd is allowed in. Rodger wishes he could go also, but public relations dictates that he be the visible family representative. So here he stands, the grieving friend but consummate host. He waits until the girls, the doctor, and nurse are seated in the side foyer and the curtains are drawn, then he motions for the doors to be opened.

The music begins, the crowd files in, many grieving friends and fellow workers, many business acquaintances, and many who are simply curious. He sees, but does not see. He hears the speeches even his own, but he does not hear. His eyes take in the whole drama, but his mind refuses. It is the first funeral he can remember caring about since his parents died in a car crash when he was sixteen. He knew nothing of death then, he knows way too much of death now. How many services like this has he attended, doing all the right things, saying all the right words? How do you manage that without any understanding of death, its imminence or finality?

The service ends with a prayer. Anna and her party are removed before the other guests according to plan. So Rodger is surprised when he exits the building to a scene of horror. Anna, Naydar and Dr. Walker are surrounded by reporters and cameramen, paparazzi, joined by the merely curious who crowd in to observe. Anna is terrified, Naydar is confused, and Dr. Walker is trying to a maneuver through the throng, answering "no comment" to every question. The limousine is blocked by the crowd. Where is the security that should be handling this? Rodger sees them pushing back against a group who appear to be picketing. He takes charge and bullies through the media using his body to stall while the women are loaded. He continues to answer every question with nothing said until the limo is around the corner, chased by the paparazzo.

To his dismay, when he arrives at the penthouse, he sees reporters and cameras camped outside. He is repulsed, furious but also perplexed as to what could be drawing so much attention. Again he fights his way to the door with polite non-answers only this time he actually listens to the questions. "How did the Benson's die? What was the true cause of death? Is it true their daughter has no memory of the happenings? What about the estate? Is there any truth to the rumor there is a challenge to the estate?" On and on they go as Rodger maneuvers his way through them. He has a flashback to picking his way through the debris toward the beach of Benkulu and the yacht. It is that memory that puts a grime smile on his face.

Up in the penthouse, Dr. Walker is administering a sedative to Anna, while Naydar is crying each time the noise from outside gains in volume.

"Do you have another syringe or two of that stuff, and is it any good?" he asks her.

"Why? Do you need some?"

"I might, but right now, I am thinking of Naydar. Do you think she might need a shot of something?"

"Right now, I think I might need a shot of something." She calls the nurse they have hired, gives her directions for treating Naydar, writes a prescription, for extra medication, then turns to Rodger. "How do I get out of here and back to my office? I have other patients."

"We need to discuss today and what comes next for the girls."

"Agreed, but not now, as I said, I have other patients. I will return after office hours,"

He is not enthused as he ponders the options. He calls someone on the phone, then sends her along with Ellen Hale, the housekeeper, to the kitchen exit where a car will take her to her office and Ms. Hale to a different neighborhood to fill the prescription. With that done, he looks around as if expecting a monster to pop out of the closet, makes himself a stiff drink, flops down in a chair and breathes.

Chapter 16

It is almost seven when Dr. Walker returns to the penthouse. She comes through the kitchen again to avoid the crowd that still mills about outside the entrance. He calls police and security, and shows his frustration at the lack of progress. The girls are subdued and shaken. The doctor examines the situation, calls the hotel restaurant and orders a meal of soup and sandwiches for the entire group. They eat and then the girls retreat back to their bedroom, and the nurse is dismissed for the night, which leaves Rodger facing Dr. Walker with no ideas.

They are considering their alternatives when the phone rings. He sighs, looks at the caller ID, and answers. Ms. Dailey reports that the office is under siege. James is holding off reporters and demands he return to the office as soon as possible. Also that Dr. Burrell has called again.

"Get her number. I will be there as soon as I can manage the situation here."

Dr. Walker listens and gathers her stuff as if to leave. He stops her. "Please, I need a favor. I need for someone I/they trust to stay with the girls until I can put things in motion."

She nods and he heads to the other room to make calls. When he returns he tells her that it will only take an hour. She looks at him amazed. He tries to talk her into accompanying them to the Benson Estate. She shakes her head.

Ms. Hale appears. Shortly after, there is a tap on the door. The security man nods at Rodger who goes into the bedroom and wakes the girls, tells them he is leaving for a bit.

He returns to the sitting area and thanks the doctor. Then the security man escorts her back to her car. She leaves wondering if they will get the girls out, and how long it will be before the media catches up with them. She gets another call from Rodger. He thanks her again, and asks if she will call the nurse telling her to prepare to stay for a while. She agrees and does as he asks.

Back in the suite, Rodger tells the girls to pack and wait for Phil. They are to do whatever Phil tells them. Then he leaves threading his way through to crowd, to his limo which takes him back to the office.

James meets him at the elevator. Talk about siege mentality. He is furious and expects Rodger to solve the problem from the elevator. First, Rodger has never seen the calm cool lawyer in such a state, and second, he has no intention of discussing anything pertaining to the developing situation in the hallway. He heads to his office with James sputtering behind. Once inside, he reminds James, "the media will be a part of whatever happens now, so let's calm down and try to figure how to put them in our corner. What about this will? Is there something there that I should know? "

"I don't know," is James' surprising answer. "It is in Carl's lock box or his safe, and only after there is a legal line of guardianship can it be opened. That is why I have been pushing so hard to have you declared Anna's legal guardian."

"What? What about *the whole company goes to charity if no descendant is alive* bit?"

"Oh, I know that is there, I wrote it. But he was very closed about some of the specifics of the rest. I feel there is a surprise there, but I am not sure."

Rodger ponders the news. "Then there could be something to the rumor of a challenge to the will?"

James lifts his hands gesturing his lack of knowledge. The two are silent as each explores his thoughts. "We have to see that document," says Rodger.

"Agreed," says James.

"So what is the next step?"

"We have Anna declared to be Anna and also declared to be impaired.That will give us temporary guardianship. It would help if someone knows where the key to Carl's lockbox is or even what the combination is to the safe."

Silence.

"Let's work on getting the medical documents in order first. Then we need to see Anna safely to the estate where she can be insulated from the morning news cycle. See if you can think of any places where the information we need might be, and draw up the necessary paperwork. I will check with Anna's doctor and with the authorities who approved the DNA. Get me a list of what documentation I need to ask for." James stares at Rodger. "Questions?" it is his tone that has James scurrying out the door to his own office.

Rodger looks at the clock. It is midnight. He is stuck in a time warp that recognizes no morning, no midday, no night, only now. He hears the crowd outside stir; a smile plays across his face. Round one. Back at his computer, research begins. It is hours before he finds what he needs. James sends the list of documents which he forwards to Dr. Walker for her approval and signature. He checks the time differential and puts in a call to Maggie.

"Its about time,"

He grins and sees her famous flying hair tossing as she berates him. "Its been a bit hectic here,"

"Yeah, I see the news. Well, I have some for you. The young man that was rescued from the same area as Anna says they are married."

"What, is this true? Where would we have to go to find out?"

"I don't know. I do know that he is picking Anna out in pictures from here, and the TV news there declaring her to be Annalisel Benson. That both helps your position and hurts it."

"Yeah," Rodger is thinking. "Maggs, who did the DNA on Anna?"

"An official of the Indonesian Government. We aren't allowed to mess with fingerprints or DNA. We have to have an official with us when we do either process, kind of smart all things considered."

"Yeah, so we know the DNA that Amur brought matched Anna's."

"What are you thinking," Maggie asks.

"I'm not sure. Have you seen or heard from Amur?"

"Not since we left Benkulu, but he was there the day before. I'm not sure I'm liking where this is going."

"Right now, it is going nowhere. It is between you and me. Right?"

"Sure, keep me in the loop please, I care about that girl."

"Maggie, you care about everybody," he laughs.

Another twist to add to the pile. He is beginning to feel as if the debris on the beach of Benkulu is nothing compared to this. Sleep, he needs sleep. James is sleeping in his office when Rodger leaves through the back entrance. He starts to go to his apartment, thinks better of it and heads to the penthouse. The crowd is as thick as ever. The housekeeper lets him in, reports on the events there, and as the sun rises, he falls into the guest room bed seeking sleep. Four hours later, he arises, heads out, hurries to his apartment to shower and change before facing the tangled mess again.

Chapter 17

First order of business is to check in with Phil. His report on the welfare of Anna and Naydar starts Rodger's day off with a bang. The nurse is the next call. She demands extra pay for dealing with the press. He is not surprised, suggests that she hang in there for two more days, and leaves this mess simmering for a while as he deals with the business that sits on his desk. This afternoon, he will accompany the Bensons to their final resting place in Utley. One more time, he thinks, one more time.

He and James push through the crowd to the waiting limousine that heads toward the funeral home. It lines up behind another limousine behind the two hearses. The solemn procession augmented by several cars filled with Benson Enterprises employees buffeted by security, heads north out of the city toward Utley and the final resting place for the Bensons. It is a quiet drive if one doesn't turn around and see the parade of media vehicles that lag behind. Rodger is in his blue suit with an expensive tie, and shoes that make him think back to Indonesia and his introduction to that country. Sneakers have new worth and meaning for him now. Somehow on this most unimaginable day, his thoughts turn to Maggie, Bobby, and Evelyn. He wonders where they are and what they might be doing. He opens the lap top from his briefcase and immerses himself in the job of running Benson Enterprises while he is still in charge.

James sits there in his expensive suit that seems a bit tight, his tie that doesn't match, and shoes that could use a polish job. He stares at the road ahead as if it is the unreadable map to his future.

The city drops behind as the procession heads toward the small town of Utley. It is a long quiet trip spent in contemplation by one and saturation by the other. Rodger wonders about his companion. He was closer to Carl than James for sure, but then James and Carl worked together before he arrived on the scene. He accepts the difference in their behaviors attributing it to their different persona. James is, was, and always has been all business, whatever is legal and good for the company, look the other way when things are really good for business, but might be not quite legal, person. In other words, Rodger sees James as a cover my butt, and watch while you hang yours out the window guy. Whatever is keeping him from engaging in conversation, Rodger welcomes. The ride is becoming the longest time free of intrusion he has had in a while.

It is late afternoon when they finally turn into the simple church cemetery and James breaks his silence. "Wonder why Carl picked this place to be buried?" he asks.

"This is the closest place to his family home," Rodger replies. "I like that it affords some amount of privacy as opposed to one of the big city plots. Don't know if Anna will find life more exciting in New York or prefer the gentle country atmosphere here. Not my decision," he says, fervently hoping it is true.

The graveside service is brief and touching. The girls are escorted out and driven off before the last prayer. The media types surrounding the area are caught off guard. Score one for the home team. Rodger and James bear the brunt of the interest when cameras realize the main attractions are in the limousine and heading away. They break up and give chase all the way back to the penthouse where the girls, housekeeper and nurse are safely tucked away only to be viewed whenever they approach a window. James wants to leave and get back to the office so he hitches a ride with his second in command of legal. Rodger hangs back. He needs to check out the estate to see if all is ready for the girls to move there whenever the time is right, at least that is what he tells James

He travels the short distance to the estate. The limo pulls into the circular drive in front of the stately Benson mansion where he is greeted by Anna, Naydar, Phil, and Dr. Walker. "Thank you for coming, Doctor. I hope this is not too big an imposition. How was your trip?" he asks the girls.

Naydar's eyes are wide and sparkling with merriment. "It was fun."

"Phil snuck us out of there slick as glass," says Anna.

"Yes," Naydar agrees, "I put on the maid's uniform and push Miss Anna in a box to the elevator down to kitchen, no one asked, no one looked. Mr. Phil, he waits in car, off we go to airport, next stop here." She claps her hands in glee.

"Are you ready to go to the cemetery?" he asks them. They sober up immediately. The group returns to the graves he left only moments ago. Again the minister repeats the service along with the closing prayer. Dr. Walker hugs the girls and everyone returns to the estate. There Anna's nanny from infancy, a Scandinavian woman, white headed, blue eyed, with an air of total confidence, waits to take over care of the two teens. While he is at the estate, Rodger asks the nanny about a safe or any other place a will might be. She leads him right to the safe. He fiddles around a bit trying to guess at passwords using names of people or places Carl might have found memorable. She watches him, eyes hooded, mouth down turned, stance somewhat disapproving.

Phil takes Dr. Walker and Rodger to the small airfield attached to the estate and flies them to the city while security shuts down all possible access to the estate grounds. The plan is for him to return and be the liaison between the estate and the city. So far so good. Dr. Walker is amused by the deception and congratulates Phil who laughs as he checks out the plane and fires up the engine. "One of the perks of knowing a few casting directors," he says. Dr. Walker says her goodbyes at the private air field where a taxi waits to take her home. Rodger joins Phil at his apartment as the two consider the next steps over a bourbon neat.

"We have to find a combination to Carl's safe," Rodger muses.

"Where do you keep that kind of information?"

Rodger thinks, looks at Phil and smiles. "We'll see. Yes, sir, we will see. This situation is worse than any video game I have ever tried to maneuver. You are one of only a few people I trust right now. Everywhere I turn, some question about someone I thought was fine pops up. So for now, it is you, me, the doctor, and maybe Dave, that is it."

"How much do you trust the Doctor Lady? How long have you known her?"

His grin relieves some tension. "I want to know how you got her to come today. I had no luck trying last night. Of course I don't have your curly hair and engaging grin, but then I am an important guy. Relax, she is being monitored as we speak. No, the doctor to whom I refer is Maggie, and I think I would trust her with my life."

Phil smiles and raises his glass for a salute. "Hear, hear. Me too."

"If you don't trust her, why let Dr. Walker know where the girls are?"

"I don't distrust her, I don't know her, and we are going to need her help starting with the paperwork on Anna's condition."

Phil purses his lips, "Why not bring Maggie in?"

"She will quickly tell you she isn't a psychiatrist. And I don't know where she is or what she is doing."

"Back to business. When you go back upstate with the girls, keep a close eye on the nanny. I want to know if she is on our team or one of the ones to watch."

"Ooo, the plot thickens. What do you know about her?"

"Only that she was an old friend of Maria's, that she was hired the week our girl was born and has been with them ever since. Even when Anna left to go to school in Switzerland, she stayed. Not sure the exact connection but that is a staunch tie. I'd say that next to Carl, she was Maria's anchor."

"Wouldn't she have said something if that wasn't Anna?"

"Right now, I don't know what to think. Watch her, charm her, see if we can believe her."

The two ease through another hour before making their way to bed. Rodger in Phil's room, Phil on the couch. When Rodger wakes, Phil is gone. He walks to the subway, takes it to another part of the city, then takes a taxi home to shower and change before he makes his appearance at the office.

Chapter 18

The weekend with its activity gives way to something resembling order. The crowd hanging around the penthouse grows noticeably smaller with each visit. He continues the established schedule, breakfast and supper at the penthouse with the housekeeper, two girls, and a bored, agitated nurse. He is sympathetic; he feels the confining stress. Ellen Hale manages best. She is familiar with the constant barrage of cameras and reporters around the building. According to her, it was a lot like this any time the Bensons were in the city. Rodger wonders if this is part of Carl choosing to vacation with family at foreign resorts, or the constant business trips. The young actresses playing Anna and Naydar are also bored, but the penthouse far eclipses their apartment. There is no complaint about the food service, and best of all, they will receive enough salary to pay their expenses for this year. They are kissing their pitiful server jobs goodbye at least for a while, as they wear the weird clothes, making sure they are visible through the windows at intervals. If the media suspects the charade, it isn't apparent.

Doctor Walker's report is in, and James has begun the guardianship petition. Phil is making daily reports concerning events at the mansion to Rodger's personal phone and only to that device. Rodger engages a private detective to check into backgrounds of all of the people involved, from the nanny, the nurse, Doctor Walker, Ms. Hale, Amur, James, Phil, yes, Phil and even himself. No one is immune from innuendo, and he wants to be in front of any information or misinformation that might be floating around. He goes as far as adding Carl and Marie's names to the list. The detective promises a preliminary report in a few days. Rodger instructs him to focus first on the people that surround Anna. He is having severe trust issues on that front.

He imagines he will receive some information on everyone but is shocked when the reports begin and reams of material find their way into his briefcase becoming his "homework". Sleep is a figment of the imagination, something remembered from long ago. His favorite report is on himself. Who knew that every mistake, every youthful escapade, every personal or business transgression is available to those who are conversant with the methods of a confidential search.

There is little in Phil's report to shock or surprise. He dates a lot of good looking women all over the world, flies anything with wings and an engine, resists gambling, and lives fugally. He is intelligent, charming, and loyal. As long as his instructions are in line with what he considers best for the company, he is right there. There are parents in Pennsylvania, a brother who is in the Air Force stationed in Colorado, and a younger sister who is still in college.

The nurse is troubling. Her employment is almost up and Rodger is troubled about her silence. According to the dossier, she has a tendency toward gossip, was relieved of two positions for releasing sensitive patient information. Rodger needs his little drama to remain in house. He is a bit surprised that Dr. Walker suggested her, but he did not give the good doctor much time to uncover a nursing option and this woman's credentials are excellent. He discusses options with Phil who suggests a quick vacation to a nice resort in the Bahamas. Rodger shakes his head, yes, that should solve that problem.

He is going through the files for Dr. Walker and the nanny. He needs to be doing his office work but somehow the reports continue to tug at his brain. Dr. Walker is as she appears, a reliable physician with a great pedigree. Her college and medical school grades and conduct are impeccable, her medical practice comes highly recommended and is growing. She is described as kind, capable, intelligent, and an asset to her patients. He is happy to pass that information along to Phil. He is beginning to feel like a match maker.

The nanny's file would be material for a novel. The detective admits the information is a bit sketchy, he has found little on her background. She seems to have some family affiliation with Maria. They were inseparable in their young adulthood. He has found pictures of the two, but mostly as he was investigating Maria. He sends the pictures of the two women to Rodger. Maria seems to be pre-teen and the nanny, Sylvie Gilbeck, he would guess to be eighteen or so. They are standing on a beach but are dressed for cooler weather. Maria has one hand covering her mouth and she is pointing with the other. Sylvie is laughing and pointing also. Whoever the photographer, he must have said or done something; the reactions seem real. In another picture the two have arms entwined and are looking at each other with huge grins as they pose on the steps of a cabin. They appear best buddies.

The third picture is one Rodger is familiar with – Carl and Maria's wedding photo. Only now he sees the figure behind Maria. It is Sylvie. If she were there, why didn't she serve as maid of honor? The rest of the file mentions a town in Sweden as Sylvie's home, no parents living, no known relatives. She graduated from school, there is no college listed, nothing else appears until she shows up again in Maria's life. There are pictures of her holding Anna as a baby and holding her hand as a toddler. She is the presence in many of Anna's school pictures. There are no more shots of Sylvie and Maria and none of Sylvie and Carl. Rodger hopes that Phil is having better luck than his detective.

He assumes the folders on Amur and James and Carl will be coming in soon. He decides that it is tomorrow's problem and returns to the work of today.

That night he dreams of Carl and Amur fishing together on the yacht he lived on in Benkulu. He awakens with a feeling of dread, the information in the files has him on edge. He arrives at the office to find a new distraction there.

"Maggie? What, when, how? Who cares, you are a sight for sore eyes. I could sure use some healing."

She smiles and gives him a hug. He has never been a hugger but who can say no to this woman, although he has certainly tried.

"You old Dodger. How are you? Are you and the girls okay? Do you have time for an old friend?"

"I will always have time for you and quite frankly, right now any friend old or not is a welcome sight. I feel like a salmon swimming against the current with no idea where I am headed. Ms. Dailey," he calls to the secretary, "Hold all calls and clear my calendar for the afternoon." He then draws Maggie into his private office and the two sit there and stare at each other. "I have news... " they both blurt out. They laugh. "You first... " again the same message at the same time.

Maggie points to herself, "Ladies first. The boy, the one I warned you of, he is still telling anyone that will listen that he and Anna were wed the day before the tsunami. I am going to tell you, I don't believe him, but I have nothing to base that on except the feeling I have as I talk with him. I did mention it to that security man from your company, that Amur. He said not to concern myself, that everything would all work out. Not too sure what he means by that but for now we have the young man, Michael, in Darwin in the hospital there. He has family in Germany and they have been contacted, but so far, no one has come or called."

Rodger shakes his head. "This is like a five headed monster, every time I think we have things handled, something new crops up."

"And the girls?"

"They are safe for now."

"Can I see them?"

"How long can you stay?"

"As long as I am needed," she says her face showing her troubled spirit.

Rodger takes her hand, "It's not that bad, it's just complicated. Come, we will go for a ride."

Now she is confused. Are they going to see the girls? If so, why doesn't he say that? She is tired, confused, and concerned, but she doesn't say anything. She rises, gathers her bag, and follows him out of the building to the garage and his gray Porsche. They climb in and he drives toward a quiet place near the banks of the Hudson. There is little conversation until they exit the vehicle and sit on a park bench overlooking the water.

"I am not sure who we can trust and who might be listening to any conversations. The girls are at the Benson mansion in Utley, New York. They are staying there with a lady who has served as Anna's nanny for years and Phil. I would take you to them, but there is a media interest in the Bensons and the girls to the point that we created a presence in the penthouse here so that everyone, except you, me, the girls and their staff, and the group at the mansion thinks they are there. Until I know who is and isn't trustworthy, I need the news folks to believe the fairy tale. I can have you stay at Phil's apartment until we can arrange for him or someone else to drive you upstate. Then you can decide if you will stay there or come back here. Does that sound reasonable?"

"Rodger, just what is going on?"

"If I knew, I would feel much better. I need Anna to regain her memory. There is a persistent rumor that there will be a challenge to the will, which we have yet to see. Anna would have the authority to open lock boxes or safes, but I don't unless she is declared incompetent which we are working on. But, Maggie, I hate to do that."

She looks at him, sighs, and nods. "Let's get me to wherever she is and let me see if I can tweak that memory. Most times, there is some leak in the block of memory and it floods back as suddenly as it disappeared. However, and I truly hope in this case, sometimes not all the memories return. I brought some pictures of Michael, and some of Naydar's mom that Amur gave me. By the way, is he on your do not trust list?"

He nods, "What is your impression?"

"I think there is something he knows and is holding back. How did he go about finding material to get Anna's DNA checked?"

"He told me not to worry about that, he would take care of it. Do you think he might have done something illicit?"

Her eyes blink as she registers what he has suggested. "I don't know. I haven't thought about that. What makes you think he might?"

"I don't want to. I suppose it could be done. Maggie, I need Anna to remember." His frustrations boil over, as he tosses a stone into the river in front of them. The day, the sky, the foliage around them is unnoticed as the improbable fights with the possible in the two heads, both of which are too tired to study.

"Lets get going, I need to see Anna and meet her nanny. If she knew her as a girl, we might find a lever to pry those memories loose."

He smiles, her protests that she isn't a psychologist are pushed out of the equation. He ponders what will be the best and easiest way to get her to Utley. First things first, it will not do for him not to take her to the penthouse and "the girls". So they leave and head there. The actresses are glad to see anyone new, and they make a great picture posing at the windows for the persistent presence in the street. The nurse is expecting her release, and is disappointed to discover she will have a bit longer in her role. Her attitude improves when she is told of the plans for her future. Maggie is left making small talk with the "inmates" while Rodger hunts up Dave and instructs him to escort Maggie to Phil's for the night then to take her tomorrow to the mansion. He is to stay with her there so that when and if she wishes to leave, he will be available. Dave has not seen the Benson estate, but he has heard about it and considers this an adventure. He has a few items that need to be finished before he gathers Maggie. Rodger returns and they leave with Dave promising to pick Maggie up within the hour.

Back at the office. Maggie and Rodger chat as they await Dave's arrival. He makes sure Ms. Dailey is within earshot when he declares how he hates that Maggie has a meeting she must attend and wishes she could stay. Maggie joins in the story, explaining that she can't at this time, but maybe on her way back. As they talk, James approaches. He stops, looks at the two, "Sorry, I didn't mean to interrupt," he says, "I must apologize, but I need a moment of your time, Rodger."

Rodger excuses himself and the two men walk toward the elevators. They speak for a while. Then James returns with Rodger and shakes Maggie's hand, thanking her for saving Anna. He heads back to the elevator which opens to reveal Dave. The men swap places, the doors close and James is gone. Dave greets Maggie as an old friend.

"Dave, would you be kind enough to drive Maggie to her friend's place, and see if there is any other way we might be of service. Dave is momentarily confused until he observes the slight nod of Rodger's head in the direction of the secretary. His eyes indicate his understanding, then taking Maggie's bag he guides her to the door. "Phil is going to be so upset that he isn't here to see you."

Then everyone is gone and Rodger is back to work. If he could be sure he wouldn't be followed, he would go with them. As it is he takes to his personal phone to let those at the estate know they should expect company.

He delves into the merger papers yet again. How did he ever think this was the greatest adventure of life? He glances at his watch. It is almost time to head to supper at the penthouse. Packing his briefcase with papers on the upcoming deal as well as files from the detective, he opens the office door. Ms. Dailey is there glancing at her watch also. "It is about that time," he observes. "Do you have an appointment?"

"Well, I do have an engagement, I am meeting a friend," she replies as she looks back to the computer and continues her task.

"Go on and shut that thing down, whatever you are doing can wait till tomorrow," he says smiling at her.

She is startled. She can't remember ever leaving early before with permission. He has always been a stickler about punching in and out on time. She closes the program, shuts the computer, has her bag, and is headed for the elevator as if she isn't sure that he won't change his mind.

Rodger wonders at her rush, but then he too can't remember ever letting an employee leave before the allotted time. He spends an hour at the penthouse eating and visiting then goes to his apartment where he spreads the paper work on the merger from hell out on the desk. He tries to call Dave but gets no answer. He would call Maggie but figures she will be in bed asleep after her journey. Three hours in, he calls it a night and stuffs the papers back into the briefcase along with the files.

Chapter 19

The phone wakes him. He wipes the sleep from his eyes and checks – five thirty, someone is up with the roosters. It is Dave. "Hi, I need to talk with you about Maggie."

"You are taking her to Utley today, aren't you?"

"Well, no, there was a change in plans."

"What? Yes, we do need to talk. What wasn't I clear about?"

"I'll meet you and explain," says Dave.

Rodger is thinking, you bet your job you will. "Okay, meet me at the penthouse for breakfast."

"No, not there, this is a private conversation"

"At the office sevenish." This is not a request.

"See you." Dave is off and Rodger is puzzled. He rushes through his morning routine, stops by to apologize to the "girls" and manages to get to the office early. He sets his briefcase down and gathers a file to examine, but before he can begin, he hears someone in the hall. He opens his door to Dave striding in with two deli bags.

"I brought us some breakfast as I remember someone saying you tend to forget packing the essentials," he quips.

Rodger grins, "And if I remember correctly your boss said you never go anywhere without food."

Dave chuckles and spreads out his feast of bacon, egg and cheese croissants, and a bag of chocolate crème puffs. Rodger shakes his head and prepares the coffee pot for brewing.

"Okay, talk," he says sitting down facing Dave.

"After we eat," Dave hedges.

Rodger frowns. "While we eat,"

"Well, I was all prepared to take Maggie over to Phil's place for the night, but she up and declares her decision to go on to Utley last night. Boss I mean I am trying to talk her out of it and have you ever crossed ideas with that woman?" Rodger's head falls back as he breaks out in laughter. Dave continues, "Anyhow, I am explaining why it will be so much better if we don't barge into them unexpected especially at night. I look over to her and she is in my car, using a cell phone to find a flight to Utley. Now," he swallows, and chugs a bit of coffee, "I know you don't want her on a commercial flight," he says the word commercial as if it is somehow nasty. "So I get on my phone and call the hanger telling them to ready a piper for flight." He observes the reaction to his statement, "Don't worry Boss, I told them I was doing a security check, and I made sure they never saw Maggie. We arrived at the destination about dusk and the estate shortly there after."

"How did that go?"

"Oh fine. The girls were ecstatic to see Maggie, and Phil was ecstatic to see anyone male. By the way, that Nanny Sylvie is a piece of work. I'm watching her watch Maggie and the girls like a lioness observe her cubs playing with a hyena. We ate, then Sylvie told, yes – I said told – Maggie she would show her to her room. I'm waiting for the explosion, when Maggie blinks, gathers the girls for a goodnight hug and follows her down the hall."

Rodger chuckles as he motions Dave to go on.

"Phil drags me out in the corridor asking what is up. He says you have called saying we would be there today. I look him in the eye and ask if he had ever crossed Maggie. Anyway, he tells me he hasn't learned anything. That Sylvie is a closed mouth witch," he glances at Rodger to make sure he understands that isn't the exact spelling. "I think he is hoping to be relieved." He pauses to chew as Rodger ponders the information so far. "But boss, this morning, you would have thought those ladies had been friends forever. They are laughing and chattering like high school chums, and it is not daybreak. I don't think I will ever understand women."

"They have something in common, they both care about Anna." Rodger points out. "Anna trusts Maggie therefore, Sylvie is much more likely to consider her an ally." He pursed his lips, "That Maggie, she is amazing. She has turned this potential stumbling block into an asset."

Just then, his personal phone rings. Phil is on the line. "Dave left us this morning," he explained, "You need to get a report from him."

"That is happening as we speak. What is going on there this morning?"

"Maggie and Sylvie have been going through all of Maria's stuff, some of Carl's, and things Anna played with as a girl. They are laying it all around the house where she can't help but see it. I have seen her stop and pause by a few objects already. Boss, we don't need to rush anything court wise. I think this might work. I watched her pick up a bracelet when she didn't think any one would see."

Rodger is listening, nodding, as Dave licks chocolate from his fingers.

"Do you need me there?" asks Phil.

"No, I need you right where you are. The information you are gathering is what we must have to make a decision here."

He sighs, "Okay, but frankly I was getting no where until Maggie showed up. I think she is what you need."

The conversation is over. Dave and Rodger turn their attention to this day. "I think I will go get some sleep and then a bit of R&R" says Dave.

"Sleep, yes. R&R will have to be tabled. I am thinking the way things are moving we might need you to do a little slight of hand concerning personnel. Stay sober and stay in touch."

Dave nods. Noises from the reception area alert them that the office is stirring. Rodger motions for Dave to follow him. He leads him to a hidden exit that goes directly to the parking garage. There they say goodbye and Dave heads to Phil's apartment and bed.

Rodger opens the office door. Ms. Dailey is putting up her purse and uncovering the computer. "How was your night?" he asks.

Her face freezes, chalk up another first for the boss. He watches as her face relaxes into a shy smile. "Could you come in and let's go through the day's assignments?"

She gathers her tablet and follows him into the office. He indicates that she should sit. "Did you have a nice night?" he repeats the question.

"Uh, yes sir," she stammers, "My friend and I went to see a Broadway show."

"Was it a good one? I hear the new one at the Drake is great."

She tenses, her face blanches. He can't remember seeing her so uncomfortable. No actually that isn't correct, he can't remember paying any attention to her at all. He looks at her as she eyes him. She is average height, salt and pepper hair done in tight curls, her dress is gray and office appropriate. She isn't stout, but she is solid. He doesn't think that yesterday he could have picked her out of a line up. He begins to consider he might not be the easiest boss to work for.

They discuss the communications that are necessary for the next stage of the merger. Then he dictates a letter to a Mid East company concerning a possible purchase of an asset there. He dismisses her with a smile which she returns.

He pulls out a file. This one is on James. As he reads, he thinks how does anyone work side by side day after day and know nothing about someone. James' wife is divorcing him. Rodger can't pull up any image of said wife. Yes, James had a "woman on the arm" at business functions, but then so did he, and he honestly can't remember what *his* "woman on the arm" looked like. The divorce is recent and expensive. He remembers the derogatory thoughts he had concerning how James was dressed at the funeral and again at the grave side service. Maybe here is the reason. All his credentials in the file are excellent. His schools are listed as is his current address and former addresses, even the addresses of his children, one in New Jersey, one in Connecticut, and one showing with two grandchildren in California. He had not known James had children much less grandchildren. They discussed business, potential business, possible business problems ad nauseam, but nothing about life out of the office. Benson Enterprises is their only point of contact.

Lunch time finds him still in deep thought. He is pondering the compartments that make up his world when Ms. Daily taps upon his door.

"Come in," he says without glancing up from his sheet.

"Sir, a Mister Shelbee would like a word. He doesn't have an appointment, but he is rather insistent. He says he is a lawyer and it is about the Benson estate."

Rodger sees her shake her head no. He smiles and answers in a tone audible in the reception area. "Sorry, I have no spare time today and would prefer to schedule an appointment when our attorney or representatives of the legal department can be present. Take his information and tell him we will work out a meeting in the next few weeks. Have the legal department look into that."

She smiles, "Yes sir, I will let him know." She shuts the door as she is relaying the unnecessary message.

It occurs to him that the atmosphere in the office is a bit different today. He can't put his finger on it exactly, but it is different.

Back to the files, he reviews James, then turns to Carl. Now here is someone he knows. He and Carl are close. It takes all of five minutes for him to understand that he knows a lot less about Carl than he thought. He knows the background, Carl's birth on the Benson Estate, the old money connections that land him at the prestigious business college only to find that his real interest is in energy production and dissemination. The argument that drives him out on his own, putting him at odds with his father, pushing him to success. What he doesn't know is that Carl is a skirt chaser. He has always considered Maria to be Carl's one and only love. Here are stories from several earlier relationships, not that they are surprising, just unknown to Rodger. Carl had been the famous young entrepreneur and geologist with the smarts and drive. It is Rodger who has the touch for business. That is the way the relationship always appeared to him, now he wonders if Carl was overseeing his every move.

Another shock comes with the pictures, here is Carl fishing on the same boat that served him as home in Benkulu and that man with him is Amur, no doubt about it, it is the scene of his dream. They seem to be beyond business chums. There are several others taken in the Mid East that include Amur. There is only one that includes Maria with Carl and Amur. There are pictures of business dinners, functions that deal with the area and tycoons from there, but the strangest to him are those that are definitely social in nature, like the one on the boat, or one that is the opening of some restaurant. He had no idea that Amur is anything but an employee to Carl. This opens his eyes and brings new perspective to the whole mess. Is Amur propelled by his devotion to the company and his continued employment, or has his journey been more personal, attached to his friendship with Carl?

Rodger holds this file as he searches for the one on Amur. He stuffs them both in his brief case. He pushes the intercom to let Ms. Dailey know he is going to be out of the office for a while. He needs time away from here, time away from her, to clear his head and think. Ms. Dailey stops him mid-sentence to tell him that James is on the line. He takes the call. They set up a time to confer in the morning. Then Rodger sneaks out through his private entrance, makes his way out of town toward upstate never noticing the car that follows him, not that they are learning much. He finds a place close to the water and sits there, staring into the flow. Occasionally, he will toss a pebble in, occasionally a sigh escapes. Here he is, back where he is in control, or so he thought. His head hurts.

Chapter 20

This is a day of new revelations and progress at the Benson Estate. Maggie is worming her way into Sylvie's confidence with each passing hour. The plan the two hatched last night to help awaken Anna's memory seems to be producing results. She has touched several pieces of her mother's jewelry, and there is a picture she keeps coming back to. They place the picture in a hallway leading toward the pool. In the photograph, Maria, swathed in her bathing suit and a wrap, holds Anna in her arms. Sylvie says Anna is three in the photo. Anna isn't happy. She is crying and holding out her arms as if she wishes to be put down. The photo is not where Anna would pass by it unless she chose to do so. So far Maggie has seen her there three times, and Sylvie has seen her there twice, once holding the picture in her hands. The two have decided not to pressure Anna, but to let her come to them. Anna is doing a good bit of what Maggie refers to as wandering. She aimlessly treks from room to room here on the main floor. She talks for a while with one of them, then is off again, sometimes accompanied by Naydar, sometimes not. She is quiet, and nervous. The slightest of sounds draws a startled reaction. She picks distractedly at her food.

It is after a lunch of soup and sandwiches during which three people talked about the weather, the flowers, and make general observations about anything and everything except the silent, white faced girl who says nothing, looks only at her plate, and seems completely unaware that they are there.

After plates are cleared, Anna leaves Naydar watching a movie and heads toward the pool. Behind her are the two middle aged stalkers taking care not to be seen. Anna again picks up the picture and holds it for a moment. She passes her hand across her forehead as if to push away a painful vision. Then she replaces the picture and strolls to the pool deck. She takes a seat on one of the aqua loungers. Maggie and Sylvie are peaking through the curtains watching. Nothing. Anna doesn't move, nothing is said, silence rules the area.

Maggie looks at Sylvie who returns the look with a shrug. They wait. About thirty minutes go by before Naydar wanders out wondering where everyone else is. As the two conspirators hear her footsteps headed their way, they flee to the back sun room. Naydar calls softly, "Anna? Maggie? Sylvie?" No answer. She looks toward the pool area and starts to turn when something stops her. It is the soft sound of tears. She crosses the concrete pool deck, listening, and stopping frequently to cast her eyes to the various areas that envelope the pool in search of the origin of the sound.

This area is a stunning architectural delight. The pool design resembles an ocean inlet, surrounded by a bee's delight of flowers and bushes that lead uphill briefly to a water feature that bubbles with soothing sounds as it delivers fresh water to the pool and in the process causes a tiny wave effect. On the hill itself are several trees two of which are fruit bearing. Over all, the effect is delightful to the senses and soothing to the soul. But, this day, the soul in question is not soothed. Anna is seated staring with unseeing eyes at the lovely area meant to please and comfort and sees only past and pain.

Naydar rushes to her side and immediately begins to coo as she strokes Anna's trembling shoulders. Anna's response is negligible. Naydar, alarmed, heads to find support. She calls out for the women who respond much quicker than she thought possible.

"What is the matter?" asks Sylvie.

"Where is Anna?" is Maggie's question.

Naydar points to the figure huddled in the luxurious lounger. The two women approach with concern and caution. Should they stay, or should Anna be given some time to come to terms. Both are convinced that Anna's memory is returning.

The three, Anna's support group unconsciously form a circle as if to guard Anna from the thoughts and memories that come flooding in. Anna sees her mom, in her favorite place at the edge of the water. Over there on the side hidden from view of the windows, is where Grandmother Benson sat when she lived here. Anna retains wisps of memories of her, none of a grandfather. The woman sat hours upon end there in the chair reading or sewing, but never spoke unless dad was home. She would speak to her son in tones that dripped honey, making it seem as if all day had been a lark. When Dad wasn't home, the only utterances were to the staff, and for Maria to get that noisy baby out of her house.

Anna wipes her shaking fingers across her face as if to change the scene. It did, the older woman disappeared and Sylvie appeared. Now was laughter, games, and lunches here. Dad is home more, spending time with them. Then sometimes, it is just her and Sylvie. Sylvie always ready to play, always within calling distance. Sylvie. Anna looks up, her tear-streaked face red, her blues eyes puffy. She reaches up her arms like in the picture. Naydar reacts toward her, but Maggie catches the arm before it can make contact. Sylvie sits down and gathers the weeping girl in her arms. They cry and rock together. Maggie motions Naydar toward the main house and they steal away leaving the two behind to grieve.

Maggie wants to talk with Anna before she calls to report, as the parameters of memories have not been probed. She feels a touch out of her depth and muses upon the idea of asking Phil to contact Dr. Walker. The longer she considers it the more logical it feels. She scouts up Phil, puts in her request and leaves the rest to him.

While Maggie and Phil are concocting the next chapter in this overcharged day's drama, Naydar is totally lost. She wants to comfort her friend but has been sent away. Maggie has disappeared to hunt for Mr. Phil leaving a bewildered Naydar pacing and wringing her hands. How to help? What should she do? Is there anyone she can turn to? And so for the second time since coming to the USA, Naydar uses her cell phone to contact her uncle. He reassures her, recommends that she go praise Allah and wait for instructions. She does as he suggests, finding the prayer most healing. She returns to the room where the four of them have spent the majority of their brief time here together and taking out a book, prepares for the next happening.

Chapter 21

In the office, the atmosphere is reserved. Perhaps because here no one knows what is happening in Utley. Phil assumes that Maggie called, and she is sure he reported the wonderful news. Here there are meetings, suggestions, three tables covered with various projects in differing stages of completion. The merger proposal with its latest correspondence occupies one table, while the three different acquisitions with correspondence and to do lists, indicating the differing stages with appropriate connections and contact numbers of all pertinent persons rested on another. Another table is set aside for the ongoing condition of the Benson estate and all its concurrent legal files. The remaining table along with the box underneath it contains Rodger's working files on all the persons involved in the Benson business, with the recent events, or in contact with Anna Benson.

Sometimes it seems that he spends most of his waking hours either working on company business or trying to provide a clear path to save the company business. Each day brings new information and the personal files continue to grow. He spent last night reviewing Carl's life. There is a distinct cord from Carl to James, and from Carl to himself. The connection with Amur is also documented, but, except for the file which contains his own information, he gets the impression something is missing. In his case, he knows everything is not listed. There are many active encounters between himself and Carl that are not included. It is a relief that the investigation is not completely invasive, but at the same time, he wonders what all is missing from the other files that have outgrown his briefcase and now reside in the box under the table.

The intercom buzzes to let him know that James has arrived. Showdown time. No more working through this alone. He is going to bring the person, who next to him, has the most to lose, up to date.

"Well, you have been busy," James comments indicating the piles on the different tables.

"Yeah, I hope you allotted a generous slot for this meeting, because I think it is time *we* put it all out there."

James' expression goes from relaxed to wary. He eyes the tables covered in files and pulls at his tie. The dark business suit hugs his waist. His hands reach to smooth his thinning hair. He is a stark contrast to the taller, leaner Rodger with his coat and tie off and the sleeves of his shirt rolled up. James looks like the consultant and Rodger the worker. Actually the picture was pretty accurate two hours ago, until over lunch alone at his desk with a new problem about one of the acquisitions, Rodger decides to make this a team effort.

He points to the tables and explains to James that he needs him to step up and help. James suggests two of the younger associates in the office. Rodger's steady stare stops him.

He pulls at the edge of his suit coat and suggests maybe Phil. With no reaction from Rodger, he asks, "Why me? Why now?"

"Because you and I have been here from the beginning, and I trust your judgment." James fidgets. Rodger watches him, then enquires, "Why not James?"

"I'm not who you think I am," is the answer.

Rodger purses his lips, glances up, scoots his chair over to the table that holds the personal files. He picks up one, opens it and begins to read.

"Full name, James Leyton Stanton, born in Ithaca on January twelfth 1980. You attended Northeast Catholic Academy graduating," here he stops and looks up at the stunned lawyer. "Shall I continue?"

"You investigated me?" James face grows red. His eyes enlarge.

"You, might want to look at this." He hands him the Rodger Madden file.

"I'm not following. You investigated yourself?" His eyes narrow, and his face pinches in. He is perplexed.

"Everybody. Look, someone is messing with the news and threatening an investigation. Rumors are flying that there will be a challenge to the estate. We don't know if or when Anna will regain her memory, and we cannot let the estate filing drag on. We need to know where Carl's will is, what other papers are locked away, and we need to know fast. Number one, we have to know who we can and can't trust, and we have to know what is out there that might come back to bite us. This is what the military calls threat assessment, don't you agree?"

James stands still, file in hand, then he bobs his head in agreement.

"Okay, then we are in this together as a team?" He asks. Again James thinks it through. Rodger smiles, good old, reliable, steady, how will this affect me, James.

Finally James pulls up a chair, loosens his tie and spreads out the closest file, Carl's. He looks at the name, looks at Rodger, grabs a pencil and pad and begins to take notes. The two partners work in silence fo a while then stop to compare notes on what they each are understanding from the files.

"Tell me what you know about the relationship between Carl and Amur," Rodger begins. He is holding Amur's file, while James has been taking down notes on Carl.

James taps the pencil on the notepad looking for the spot he wants. There it is, "He first met Amur in Iraq when he was doing some work for the department of defense. There isn't anything here about what his assignment was, only that it was classified."

Rodger checks, "That is right, Amur was also working with the DOD. He shows up as an asset in the area. At the completion of the assignment, Amur is hired on as the chief of security for Benson in the Middle East region."

"Pretty interesting position for a new hire, wouldn't you say?"

James looks at Rodger with a growing sense of dread. He looks back at Carl's file, "What am I missing?"

Rodger shakes his head. "Don't know, but I am missing it too. They appear to have hit it off almost instantly unless there is another contact we missed. Here is a picture of them fishing off the yacht, another at a social function."

"Wait," James pulls out several pictures from Carl's file. They show Carl and Maria at various parties. There are three that show Carl with Amur at what is a social function. Do you have these in that file?"

"Yes," Rodger pulls them out.

"Okay, do you see Maria anywhere?"

He examines them again looking more closely into the background. "No," is his puzzled answer. "There is a woman here but she seems to be with Amur. See?" He pushes the file down the table. James looks at it, finds the same woman in his photos and circles her. He reaches into a drawer, grasps a magnifier and examines the pictures once again. He looks up with a strange gleam in his eye.

Rodger grabs the magnifier, checks the photo, and looks up at James. "Naydar? No, can't be, she is too young. This was taken years ago. Is there a date on the picture?" He is turning the photos over looking for a date, while James begins to check the file for any indication as to what the function is, where it might have been held, and what the two men are doing there.

The phone breaks the search. It is his private line. Maggie is practically yelling, "She remembers, she remembers. It is all coming back." The men can hear excited laughter and giggles galore in the background.

Naydar snatches the phone, "Mr. Rodger, wonderful day, she knows me. We talk of her parents. I so happy."

There is an obvious struggle for the phone, Phil wins, "Boss, you heard? We are relieved and waiting. What comes next."

"Don't push her, let her deal with this quietly and at her own speed. We will have questions but not just yet. Meanwhile, I will call Dave and make plans to join you soon." As if on a cue, the office phone rings.

Ms. Dailey informs him that the lawyer Mr. Shelbee is here and demanding an audience.

James smiles and heads to the door before Rodger has time to digest the information or to replace his phone.

"You deal with that, I'll deal with this," he says, indicated the man in the reception area. Rodger agrees.

James retires to his office with the aforementioned lawyer. He takes down a running record of their conversation without the intruder aware that everything he says is being recorded.

Rodger calls Dave, gets the report on the media activities, and sets up a plan to bring the girls back to the penthouse. By tomorrow, if all goes well, Anna and Naydar will be in the city, the two doppelgangers and their "nurse" will be at the Benson's Utley Estate hopefully with a large segment of the media stuck outside the gates. Maggie will be with Phil and the girls. If we pull this off, he thinks grimly, I will never believe a news cast again.

The wheels turn, as smiling confident James knocks on the door jam and asks permission to enter. Rodger nods as he makes a note of the time, approximating when he anticipates the assignment's completion and results being reported. James winks at Ms. Dailey which leads to an eyebrow raise by Rodger. "The divorce?"

"The main reason for it," James answers. "You can't know how relieved I am that it is out in the open, and Claire and I don't have to slip around."

"If it is for my benefit, I think you worried for no reason." He grimaces and adds, "I doubt I would have noticed or cared."

"You wouldn't," agreed Claire Dailey, with a grin.

"Okay, James might as will head inside and catch me up on what is going on with the legal department. Ms. Daily bring your tablet and take notes, or film or whatever. God, I am getting old."

The three retreat into the office where James starts but Rodger cuts him off, explaining the now existing plans to exchange the groups as well as to retire the nurse, and he asks if either of them has any ideas for adding on or eliminating parts of the plan before he gives the word to go. Ms. Dailey's mouth is open as she and James stare at each other. They are all walking on unfamiliar ground. All three go over the extraction plan and agree, then Rodger calls to set it all in motion.

Everyone takes a deep breath and releases that plan to turn to the next problem. Mr. Shelbee, and his accusations. James has the conversation on tape, but Rodger asks for the short version. He nods and begins, "Well, it seems Mr. Shelbee has been hired to represent the interests of one Michael Gilbeck who claims to be the husband of Annalisel Benson. He claims they married the evening before the tsunami and were together, on the beach, alone when they were separated by the wave of the tsunami. He heard that she is safe and in the hands of her father's company officials, who are not necessarily people who would have her best interest at heart. He demands that we bring his client here, reunite him with his wife so that he can take care of her physically and make sure her interests in the company are being honored."

Now even Rodger's mouth is hanging open. He shakes his head as if to shake off what he has heard. He opens his mouth but nothing comes out. Everyone is silent as everyone thinks about what is coming up. Rodger straightens. Light returns to his eyes, his mouth hardens, and his shoulders straighten. He looks at the pair in front of him, "I need a safe house for two women."

Ms. Dailey shakes her head. "They can stay with me if you trust me; it will not be traceable."

"First, who are we talking about, and second will they be more comfortable without Claire." James pauses as both start to speak at the same time, "Claire can spend a few evenings with me. When do we need to have all this done?"

Rodger says "Now." He goes to the phone to call Phil and warns about the change in plans. He hands the phone to the housekeeper and Rodger explains the upcoming swap to her while James calls Dave bringing him up to date and setting the wheels in motion. Dave sets out as soon as possible. Next call is to Maggie. She is brought up to date and the new plan is agreed upon. Ms. Dailey heads home to clean, pack and wait for the next step. Rodger and James look at each other, take down another file, and pretend to work while they wait for their part of the plan to begin.

Chapter 22

As soon as the call comes from Dave to say he is approaching the Estate, Rodger calls Maggie. Assured that all is in place for their Secret Mission as he is now referring to this, Rodger and James leave the office with a security detail involving four vehicles. They pull up in front of the Penthouse causing quite a stir. News organizations who have few assets available are frantically on their phones calling home offices, attempting to beef up the available personal. Those who monitor the building off site are scurrying around to find physical bodies to join the gathering.

Rodger exits the second car and heads inside while James helps to set up a perimeter manned by Benson Enterprise officers. Within minutes Rodger reappears with the girls and the nurse. All heads are covered and the apparel is generic. Anna, head down is ushered into Rodger's car. Naydar quickly joins her as the nurse is placed in the third car. James and Rodger confer for a while, then they climb into cars, James in the lead car Rodger with the two girls The security detail heads to the vehicles and everyone, including all the media who had cars available head out. The pace is normal not rushed, the following media are up to the task. The trip becomes a parade.

Hours later, the stream of vehicles pulls into the cemetery in Utley, without anyone taking notice of the blue sedan heading in the opposite direction as Dave drives Maggie and Sylvie toward the city. Again the security detail forms a barrier between their cars and the nosy press. Anna and Naydar exit, walk to the gravesite to pay their respects. It is quick, and even the media is reluctant to get too close. They reenter the cars, drive to the estate and disembark, the press stopping well behind the gates of the estate. The two girls, a woman in nurses garb, and the two men enter. The remaining detail with the exception of the second car, start up engines and exit. Thirty minutes pass, Rodger returns to his car with James, and they leave the estate.

When they approach the gate, a spokesman for the collected press waves the car down. It stops and Rodger comes over to chat.

"Hello, what can I do for you?"

"Why is Miss Benson here,"

"She wanted to come to her parent's home for a while. She will return to the city and the business in a day or so. She needs some down time to be alone. You can respect that considering all she has been through lately, can't you?"

"What is going on with the estate?"

"Have papers been filed?"

"Any truth to the rumor that a challenge to the estate has been made?"

The questions fly. He smiles and answers with answers that say nothing. He stands for a while, wraps his coat more securely as if he is chilled, then holds up his hands, "If you don't mind, could any further question be sent to the offices? We can answer you easier and more efficiently from there. I'll alert the public information department to expect your concerns, and we will get back to you as soon as we can. Thank you for your patience." And with a wave of his hand, Rodger leaves them, enters his car, and returns to the city.

"You should have been a lawyer," comments James, grinning at his partner. "That was the best say everything, without saying anything speech I have ever been party to. Good job."

"I'd like to tell them where to stick it, but we can't afford enemies at this point. Do you think any of them have a clue what we are doing?"

"Nope, I always considered you a bit of a conniver, but man, you are also a director par excellence. That was slick."

"Yes, if no one sniffs it out. What is your impression of the Michael Gilbeck situation?"

"I don't know what to make of it. I can't imagine Anna getting married without a prenup. I can't see Carl allowing it."

"What if he didn't know until it was a done deed? How old is Anna?"

"She graduated from high school and enrolled in college, an Austrian college I believe, but I really can't see her not telling her parents about an upcoming marriage, especially Maria. And Maria would never keep a secret like that from Carl. No, this smells fishy, but we will have to wait it out and see. Maybe the nanny knows something, or the housekeeper. They both seem to have a relationship with Anna."

"They would have a better relationship than I do," mutters Rodger.

"Neither of us lived up to the uncle status, but I have to say, since the tragedy, you have really stepped up for that girl, and I believe she trusts you as much or more than anyone else."

Rodger's wry smile belies the warmth that invades his being. "I had no choice. Hopefully, I will do a bit better going forward. Wait a minute, isn't Sylvie's last name Gilbeck? How far out are we and is anyone following?"

Assured that they were quite alone on the road, Rodger calls Maggie. "Where are you?" he asks. She informs him that they are approaching Ms. Dailey's apartment with in ten minutes. "I will try to get there sometime tonight. As always, there is a bit of work to be done yet." The car is supposed to be secure, but at this point, he doesn't trust anyone who doesn't have a file in his box, and only some of those who do.

The car drops the two in front of the building, they take the elevator to the top floor and from there, James retreats to his office making calls on several ongoing projects, and he calls Maggie.

"Is Sylvie with you?"

"Yes," she answers puzzled.

"Is Ms. Dailey there?"

"Yes, she is explaining everything and then she is planning on leaving. She ordered dinner for us, such a sweet, thoughtful lady."

"Call me as soon as she leaves."

Chapter 23

While he plays dodgeball with the press and faces down the Michael Gilbeck situation, the group at the estate is working on introductions. The nurse and Phil are the only ones who know all the players gathered in the large sitting room. She walks to Anna and shakes hands with her then with Naydar. The two imposters merely gawk at the girls they have spent weeks imitating. Phil nods at the gathering, clears his throat, and begins. "Anna, Naydar, meet Alicia and Willow." He begins and realizes that though each sort of knows what is going on, each sort of doesn't. "We hired these ladies, er actresses to portray, play you while you were up here so that the media would leave you alone. I think it worked thanks in big part to the excellent performances, especially today." He paused and eyed the "ladies" before him. No one speaks.

Phil coughs and starts again. "Ladies, this farce is almost over. We will all stay here for a few days, no more than a week and then go to the next phase."

"Great," says the nurse, "I am getting stir crazy. It's been a while since I have talked to anyone except for you and Mrs. Hale. I can't get out of here soon enough."

"Well, the complication is that we would want you, all of you to avoid mentioning this little episode in your life for a while."

"What!" she sputters. "Just how long do you intend we not say anything?"

"We would prefer forever, but there is a reward for remaining silent for at least five years."

Alicia looks up at the word reward, but it is Willow who asks, "What sort of reward? Over and above the salaries we were promised?"

"The salaries are yours as soon as the girls return to the city. Ms. Felt, you will not have to wait that long, you will head to the Bahamas and the resort as we promised. However we would be grateful if you managed to also restrain from comment for a while. For all of you, we will help you in your profession as an act of courtesy. There will be time to go over all of the directives when your time here is done. Meanwhile, there is a lovely estate, lots of room, all sorts of rooms, activity rooms, a library, and an indoor pool. You are expected to make yourselves at home. The only requirement is there will be no contact outside of the home. Surely we can ask that of you for a week?" Phil smiles again.

He watches as the three absorb what he told them and sees reactions on the faces. The nurse is okay, not enthusiastic but okay. Alicia is intrigued, but Willow is reviewing restrictions in her head. He decides she can't be much of an actress if she is this easily read. So what is her hook?

"One week?" asks Willow.

"Give or take a day," Phil answers watching her closely.

"Can I have access to a typewriter?"

Phil counters, "How about pencil and paper?"

She thinks about it and nods.

Anna has been silent throughout this whole exchange. Now she sits straighter, looks at the two and says in a calm gentle tone, "Thank you for what you have done. Because of you, I was able to spend the last two weeks here recovering from wounds and absorbing my parent's deaths in private. Because of you, my grief was mine to share only with those left who love me," she squeezes Naydar's hand. "It is something I will never forget. You have access to me at any time. This is my promise to you."

Naydar stands up, waltzes over to Willow and kisses her on the check then repeats the action with Alicia. "I can offer you nothing but my gratitude and my promise to hold you in prayers forever." She giggles and blushes and everyone laughs. With the tension broken, talk starts and goes on till Phil excuses himself to get out of the hen party. The housekeeper asks him about meals, he points to the sitting room and suggests she ask them when and if they ever stop giggling. She smiles, nods and slips out into the kitchen. He retreats to the office, makes himself a strong drink, and considers if he ever wants to marry. By supper time, the house is one great slumber party plus one.

The girls are playing games, talking about clothes, movies, schools in the U.S. versus those in Europe, anything and everything but current affairs and what the future held.

He plans his next move to get Mrs. Felt out of the country to her Bahama vacation, and then maybe a cushy job with a family in South America. Maybe a nice little vacation for the other two with promises of financial assistance or professional assistance in the future. He gets two phone calls. One from Dave who is bored and wants to talk. And one from Gloria Walker who wants to know where he is and when he might be coming back. She misses him or so she says. Lord, he wants to believe her, but she is a doctor and he is a mere airplane jockey. That call lasts for an hour, and then he checks on the rest of the company. The girls are yawning and agree when he suggests they finish the game they are playing tomorrow. Mrs. Felt was shown to her room over an hour ago. The housekeeper ushers the two newest members of the house to their accommodations then disappears. Phil, as he has every night since coming here, walks through the house checking entrances, windows, and finally checks the cable and internet access. There is one hit. He follows the trail that leads to Naydar's room. There he discovers her with a cell phone. When he asks, she says her uncle gave it to her before she left Indonesia. He smiles, retreats, calls Rodger whose phone is offline. He leaves a message then goes to his bed and worries. It will be great to have this behind him and be back up in the sky where you can see what is coming at you.

Chapter 24

There is supper on the table by the time Rodger makes it to Claire Dailey's apartment. Maggie answers the door and ushers him in. The atmosphere is cordial, but fractured. Maggie tries to straddle the buddy chair for each of the others. It is clear that Sylvie trusts her but not him, and he is not too sure about Sylvie which seems strange to Maggie. There is something, definitely, something, going on that she knows nothing about. They suffer through a very stilted dinner, Maggie trying to guide the conversation with the other two circling every word. They all retreat to the living area where Rodger pours each a glass of wine, then asks, "Ms. Gilbeck, might I speak with you in private?"

"Ms. Burrell can hear anything you have to say to me," is the guarded reply.

"Okay," he puts down his glass, walks to the entrance where he gathers his briefcase, opens it, and withdraws a paper. "Do you know a Michael Gilbeck?" he asks.

"Miguel?" she answers. "Yes, but what has he to do with anyone here?"

"Michael, not Miguel."

"They are one. Miguel is my name for him"

He frowns then continues. "I need to know his connections to people here. According to his lawyer, Mr. Gilbeck married Anna Benson the day before the tsunami, is her legal husband and therefore legal guardian. He wishes to represent her in all medical and business decisions."

"What?" comes from both females at the exact same moment.

"Is this the boy I told you about that was in the tsunami?" asks Maggie.

"She would not have married without her parent's consent, and she couldn't have married him. He's her cousin," is Sylvia's surprising comment.

"What?" now it is Rodger and Maggie whose mouths fly open.

"This is my boy, my son," states Sylvie. "Where is he? Is he all right? You say he was in the tsunami, how.. " Her hands, shaking with emotion, guard her face. As she flops into the sofa, Maggie rushes to her side and gathers the stiff body into her arms as best she can. Sylvie, so used to being alone with any and all concerns, finds it hard now to accept Maggie's embrace.

"I was eighteen, right out of school when I became pregnant. My family would not accept the situation. I was sent away to relatives in Germany who took me in and supported me through the birth. Then they too sent me away. The child, a boy I named Miguel, was sent to a childless cousin who raised him. He was called Michael. So far as I know, no one told him of me or the circumstances of his birth. Maria and I are cousins, he and Anna are cousins. No one in the family would approve of this or allow it, especially Maria. Something is wrong, you have to have the wrong person." Her head drops, the tears trickle.

Rodger has known this woman, albeit only in passing, for years now. He has never seen her show, much less share, any emotion at all, not toward Maria, nor Carl, nor anyone except the small bit that belonged only to Anna.

Maggie soothes, as much as she is allowed to. "He is fine or was the last I saw him. He was brought in only a day before Anna left to come here. We sent him out to Australia with the group that was in the best shape. I followed and was tending him until our group turned the patients we had over to the hospital in Darwin. He and Anna are the reasons I decided I need to be here."

"Okay," Rodger purses his lips, "At least Anna's memory has returned and she will be able to tell us about the young man. Naydar repudiates the idea of a marriage, but then she was working as a maid for the Benson's and may not have known about their private matters."

At this Sylvie bristles. She glares at him and retorts, "She is much more likely to know than Mr. Benson. Those two girls share a bond like few I have seen, they remind me of Maria and myself when we were young. She would know."

He runs his fingers through his hair, walks about the room, shaking his head. He has no idea what to say now, and he remains quiet. Then he asks, "Sylvie, have you ever seen your son?"

She shakes her head no.

Maggie's face twists into sadness. Her tender eyes reflect her concern. "He is a good looking young man. I didn't spend that much time with him, but what I saw, he just seemed angry, upset, and unsure. I hoped that he was somehow a part of Anna's life to help her memory. She didn't mention him yesterday. However, yesterday was extremely emotional. It was her first return of memory. As she progresses, more memories will flood her psyche. I am way out of my league here. I strongly suggest a visit from her psychiatrist. Has she been contacted?"

"Not yet." Rodger is in deep thought. Should he bring the girls back now? Let them wrestle with memory return where they are? It is late, it has been a tiring day, surely tomorrow will bring clearer thoughts.

He makes his farewell speeches to both ladies, promises to call first thing tomorrow and leaves for a night of funneling possible scenarios through his whirling brain.

His first reaction in the clarity of the morning is to check with Phil who answers the call immediately. "What's up, boss?"

"How are things going there?"

"Well, except I for feeling like I'm stuck in a nunnery, fine. Why?"

"I need for you to talk with Naydar and Anna separately and alone. Would that be possible?"

"Sure. By the way, did you get my message about Naydar and her phone?"

"No. What about Naydar and a phone? I thought we decided against letting any of the girls have outside contacts."

"That is my understanding, but last night after everyone went to bed, I traced an internet connection to her room. She had a phone and was talking to someone. I asked who, and she said her uncle gave her the phone before she left Indonesia. I didn't know what to do without contacting you, so I called, and left a message. Who is her uncle? I thought all her family died in the storm?"

The Wave Effect 129

"So did I. One more tangle to unravel. We have a young man who insists that he is Anna's husband and wants to take over her care both physically and legally. We need to find out if there is any truth to this. Sylvie says Naydar would know if there had been a marriage, and she said no when this first came to our attention. These rumors of a challenge to the estate have to be coming from somewhere. If not here, then where?"

"Maybe it is speculation. Slow news day, etcetera."

"Maybe." Rodger sounds doubtful. "Have you heard anything from Dr. Walker?"

"Uh, yes, as a matter of fact, I talked to her last night. She called to check on the girls. Boss, should I tell her about the breakthrough or not?"

"Mention it and see what she says. If she suggests seeing the girls, especially Anna, try to put her off until next week. We might wind up moving things forward a bit, but I would rather wait a few more days. How is the crowd at the gates?"

"They are still there, bored, speculation is rampart. They aren't leaving. The main topic of conversation is the rumor of a challenge. They are wondering from where said challenge might come and by whom. Others are wondering what happens to Benson Enterprises if Anna is forced out. Boss, what does happen?"

"We will have to look at all the papers, especially everything in Carl's safety deposit box and whatever is in the safe there. You might spend some time trying to come up with possible combinations to that safe. James and I tried everything we could think of and no go."

"Okay, do you want me to ask Anna?"

"Not yet, maybe when we are a bit better informed. Right now just rock on and call the doctor. Set up a time later this week or first of next. We need to get ahead of whatever is going on. Keep a close eye on Naydar. If you can find an opening, ask who her uncle might be. And if she leaves that phone lying around, see if you can check who is calling and where the call is originating. That is all I have for now. Whatever happens, keep us informed. Oh, and thanks, Phil."

Phil is stunned. He can't remember ever being thanked for doing his job. "Sure thing, I'll let you know whatever I find out. You going in today?"

"Oh sure, acquisition paperwork due in court Thursday. There might be a vacation coming when all this is finalized. Want to be in the cockpit? Be thinking of someplace quiet."

Somewhere during the night, ideas formed in his mind and with the sunlight comes a fresh attitude and new approaches. Rodger heads into the office with renewed energy. He is the first there as usual, and the first call is to James. He and Claire are on their way to the apartment to share breakfast with Maggie and Sylvie. Rodger is invited and accepts. Within thirty minutes, the food and the group gather in Claire's small apartment.

"Sylvie and I have been talking, we think it is time to gather everyone and see where we are and where we need to go."

"Again Dr. Burrell, we think alike. I was in the process of doing just that. James, please inform your assistant in legal, the head of public information, and let's see, there will be you and me—"

"Have you considered you might need to call Amur in for a part of this meeting?" asks Maggie. "I assume you have the capacity to do a conference call with him wherever he is."

Rodger's smile is a bit condescending, as he nods briefly in her direction before finishing his thought. "Phil is out of the circuit at the moment since we need him at Utley. Is there anyone else we need to call in?" he is looking at James.

"What about our detective or Dave?"

"Whoa, whoa, whoa, are Sylvie, Claire, Dr. Walker or I a part of this?"

"We are planning on keeping you informed as to what our course of action might be, but right now this is a business decision."

"Right! And we will be in the way with all our knitting and stuff! You conceited oaf. How dare you! First things first. You need help with information, correct? Are *you* going to talk to Anna? You think she is going to tell you the combination to that safe? Or do you just plan to blow it apart? And Naydar, how do you intend to approach her? The two girls have more answers you need than your whole legal

The Wave Effect 131

department, but who are we to be involved? I'm an out of place doctor, and Sylvie is the one remaining person who has been a stable part of this girl's life from conception. Dr. Walker is only her psychiatrist, she wouldn't be of any help."

"Come on Maggie, all of you are great help. We couldn't have gotten this far without you ladies, but now its time for the business side to be front and center, can't you see that?"

Had Maggie's glare been daggers, Rodger would be lying dead on the floor.

James cleared his throat.

"Before you utter a single syllable, James Stanton, you better think hard," says Claire Dailey.

Sylvie is over in a corner, a smug look covering her face. Maggie stomps out of the room and heads to the bedroom.

"Where are you going," Rodger's voice has a definite edge to it.

"Home," retorts Maggie, "Back to Melbourne. You remember Melbourne?"

"Not really," he mutters, "I never got that far."

Maggie can be heard through the slammed door talking on her phone. She has her bag in her hand upon her return. "Thanks for the accommodations Claire, I'll call a cab and head for the airport."

"Nonsense, I'll drive you,"

"Oh, no, you are due at the office in twenty minutes," counters her boss. "James, we better be on our way."

"I'll be taking a day off today, boss," Claire begins.

"Don't push this," Rodger warns.

"I have over 300 vacation days built up. Think I am taking one."

"Can she do that without notice?" Rodger turns to James.

"Oh no, I am totally out of this one." James backs up and looks down.

Claire and Maggie walk out the door. Instantly the two men's eyes widened in total disbelief. "I remember why I am divorced," says Rodger, and James nods.

Within minutes Sylvie is left by herself staring at the wall and wondering what comes next.

Chapter 25

The men are ten minutes out from the office when James remembers that Sylvie has been left to her own devices in New York City. "Maybe we better head back and pick up Sylvie. She does have information we are going to need and—"

"You want to go back? Fine. Drop me off at the office first. I have had about as much interaction with the female gender as I can handle this morning." Rodger is fuming. His temperament is not to blow up in this manner. James ascribes the reaction to the tensions of the current situation and the altercation. However, he has seen Rodger under stress and never before has he witnessed this sort of explosion. The cold, calculating COO of Benson Enterprises is having a very human melt down in face of opposition. This is new and somewhat interesting to James. He is used to his coworker flying off on tangents but never becoming emotional involved in whatever decision he made.

The car stops at the back entrance of the office and Rodger climbs out, slamming the door behind him. He leaves without a backward glance, disappearing into the building.

James climbs out of the passenger side of the vehicle, reenters on the driver's side, looks to make sure the keys are there, locks the car, pockets the keys, calls a cab and returns to Claire's. There he and Sylvie indulge in a nice informative conversation about the coming visit by her son and possible legalities Anna faces.

As the men shake out their differences, Claire drives Maggie about New York as the two vent their frustrations. Maggie thinks they are headed straight to the airport, but Claire is taking the longest route possible, the heavy traffic helping her cause. They talk about the male attitude, the difficulties women have being heard, the seeming set against women in the justice arena, which gives Claire her opening, "I sure hate seeing you leave, Anna is going to need you here."

"She has Sylvie."

"Yes, and if I could be sure Sylvie was as impartial as I feel you are, I would feel better about that."

"Humf," snorts Maggie as the airport comes into view.

"Are you going back today?"

"If I can get a ticket."

"Sure you don't want to discuss Anna's situation with Dr. Walker before you leave? I mean, I can tell her what you said happened when Anna regained her memory, but it probably wouldn't be the same as a professional's description."

"There is always Sylvie,"

"I guess. I would wish she were a bit more forthcoming. You have to drag ever tidbit of information out of that woman's mouth, and I doubt the guys," this is said with dripping sarcasm, "will take the time."

Maggie looks at her and succumbs. "Okay, turn around, we will go back and help Anna."

Claire grins, "And Naydar. Once Anna is established, those rats might ship her right back home to survive the best way she could."

At that Maggie's eyes flash and her lips form a definite sneer. "Oh, let them try. Let them try."

James is back in his office and working on the estate when Rodger appears at the door. "We are going to need Maggie aren't we?"

"To clear up this mess and make what is happening here relate to what Anna has been though there, yes, we are."

"I'd like to blame my actions on lack of sleep, but I never had much faith in women's abilities in the work place. Maybe I should be seeing the shrink instead of Anna." He grimaces. "Now, how do I get her back here?"

"Maybe she hasn't left yet. Have you called?"

"Nope." He takes a deep breath and retreats to the privacy of his office. James stares at the door for a while before he palms his personal phone and texts: *incoming bombshell.* The instant reply is: *bring it on, she is ready.* He chuckles, raises his eyes towards the COO office door and resumes his work. He would give a lot to be privy to the telephone conversation going on in there.

"Dr. Burrell, if you are still in New York I would appreciate you reconsidering your return home. It seems that I misspoke. We will need you to provide information and a bridge from Anna's experiences in Indonesia and what has happened here. I know you care deeply for the girls and would want to be here for them. I will attempt to make your stay as least tasking as I can."

There is a period of silence on the other end. He tries again, "I know I can be a bit difficult at times, but we have worked successfully before, and I feel we can do so again." He pauses. It has been a while since he has apologized, he isn't sure he remembers how it is done. "Come on Maggie, I am sorry."

"Magic word Rodger. I will stay for a while and we will try to get justice for both Anna and Naydar."

Naydar? He strains his brain trying to figure out what she might mean. "Whatever we need to do," he agrees. "Lets set up a conference with everyone involved as soon as we can get the schedule figured out."

"I think you might want to work on scheduling, but it might be better if the girls are back in town so that we can bring them in if necessary. It might take a day or so to get it on Dr. Walker's appointment book. Meanwhile, do you think we need to get Amur here? By the way, is that his first or last name?"

"First. Last is Saluar. I... you might be right. I'll have him called and told to report. Thanks." this last remark is soft and sincere.

"Don't mention it. I came to help Anna; I shouldn't leave until that task is finished."

"We will try to make that decision as painless as possible." He clicks off the phone, blows a huge sigh of relief, returns to his desk and the proposed merger papers sitting there since morning. He checks the time, buzzes the intercom only to realize Ms. Dailey is not at her desk, calls the next in line and puts in a request to have Amur notified that his presence is needed in New York. Then he calls Phil asking that he contact Dr. Walker and set a conference time with her and suggests they move up the transfer of the girls to the city to the end of this week. He puts up his phone, thinks briefly of where he would really like to put it, smiles, then sits down to resume his work.

Chapter 26

The next few days pass with little conversation between the Benson Enterprise executives and the women hanging out in Claire Dailey's apartment. Claire has returned home and also to work. She limits her exposure to both her boss and her lover to what's necessary to get the work done.

Amur has answered the call and will be reporting to James on Monday morning. The estate probate conference is set to happen on Thursday after a planned therapy session with Anna on Tuesday afternoon. The plan to reintroduce the girls to New York will happen on Saturday, and Dave will depart for Utley on Sunday to remove the two imposters on Monday. Rodger, Anna, and James will host a short news briefing on Monday to give the press a report on Anna's health, minus the psychological part, and a general report on the health of Benson Enterprises. They anticipate questions concerning the upcoming legalities involving the estate.

Rodger considers if he should go get the girls himself or send someone from the company. He asks James who suggests he run it by Claire. She suggests he run it by the other two ladies. Not the answer he wanted or expected, but it would be a chance to regain some standing, so he calls. Maggie says she will be at home for a while if he needs to come by. He consults with James on what is still needed for the estate filing and when they will have to officially admit they don't have it. He glances again at the personal files of Claire, Sylvie, Maggie, and Amur. He tucks them into his briefcase before leaving for the apartment.

Sylvie is the one who answers the door, which for some gut reason he finds strange. They all exchange pleasantries then Maggie invites him to be seated while Sylvie mixes drinks. Once in place, Rodger clears his throat and begins, "As you know, we have decided to bring the girls back to the city Saturday and hold a press conference on Monday. Anna will see Dr. Walker on Tuesday and we will all

The Wave Effect 137

gather to go through what we foresee as problems that might arise between the filing of the estate and the declaration of Anna as sole heir. I have come to ask your advice. Should I go to bring the girls to the city, or would it be better is we sent a security team?"

"Are you sure this is what you need our advice about?" Maggie questions. "I'd think there might be other considerations more pressing, like for instance if we have any idea where the will is."

"Sylvie already told me it was in the safe at Utley. But we have no idea what the combination to the safe is. I haven't asked Anna yet. I was giving her a bit of time to get herself together, but time is running out. If you have any ideas, I am willing to listen. And also, if you have any idea of the connection Amur brings to the table or what her," he nods toward Sylvie, "son is planning to throw at us, or why the company that was so eager for a merger is backing away."

His hands cover his face and for the first time, Maggie notices the dark circles under his eyes, the obvious fatigue around his mouth, and the slumping shoulders. She had not seen him this lost since the beginning days in Indonesia.The Burrell compassion wins out. She looks toward Sylvie for the okay and then slides closer to him.

"We have the combination. Sylvie will help with her son, who is going to have a time trying to deal with his own situation when he discovers the truth about his past. That leaves Amur. I know nothing about how he fits into this puzzle, do you?"

Rodger sits as her words flow over him, soothing and comforting. He closes his eyes and breaths. "Wait, what do you mean you have the combination?" He jerks to face her.

"I mean that Sylvie knows the combination to the safe. She has always had that information. Are you expediting her son's arrival here?"

"Uh, yes, I think. That is what the legal department is dealing with in conjunction with his lawyer. Why didn't you tell me you knew the combination to the safe?" He turns to Sylvie in confusion and disbelief.

"You never asked me," she answers.

Maggie shakes her head and grins, "If I know you, Rodger, you never gave a thought that a nanny would have intimate knowledge about Carl and Maria's concerns. You do realize, your prejudices are catching up with you?"

He frowns at Maggie then focuses on Sylvie. "Okay, why would a couple as wealthy and powerful as the Benson's give that sort of information to any member of their staff? Their lawyer maybe, but their nanny? Come on, it makes no sense."

Sylvie stands, gathers her light sweater closer about her and glares. "If you were talking about Carl, you would be right. He would never have given this information to me. But Maria? She is my cousin, we are, were, as close as sisters. She knew I would always take care of Anna."

He observes her in silence, then nods, "I still don't understand why James was not a party to that information."

Sylvie shrugs.

Rodger sighs. Deep in thought, he rises and begins to pace. "If we take the papers from the safe to which only you know the combination, we rely on your word to back up Anna's identification, and it is your son making the claim against the estate, the court is going to fry you."

Her chin raises, her shoulders square, "I am not now, or ever have been afraid of what anyone else thinks. Anna is like my own. I have been a part of her life since she was an infant. My son, now him I haven't seen since the day he was born. They took him from me, and made sure I would not repeat that mistake. Anna is the only child I will ever have." Her eyes fill, but not a drop escapes. The stern Swedish features seem formed in stone.

Maggie is torn, the two both show such needs, and she is a giver, but she knows not how to give. Therefore, she sits and watches.

"Did Carl know of your connection with Maria?" Rodger stops, checks her body language.

Sylvie shakes her head yes, but stiffly. Rodger seizes on her reluctance, "He sort of knew? Knew some, but not all?" He questions.

"He knew we were kin, and we were close as girls. He never knew about Miquel or that I could never have children. He thought Maria was giving me a job out of pity. He never knew how much she needed me to make her feel at home, to help her with his family particularly that mother of his, and to be her sounding board." Sylvie shakes her head, she resumes her place on the sofa and stares into space. Maggie reaches toward her but stops before contact is made. Rodger continues to pace.

"That safe is Maria's or Carl's?" He asks.

"Both I think" her voice is devoid of any emotion. It is as if all energy has drained from her system, leaving a shell of womanhood there.

"If the safe belongs to both of them, then any secret materials will be elsewhere wouldn't they?" Maggie comments. "Is there somewhere else we need to look to find the bottom of this mystery?"

Sylvie comes to as if regaining a purpose, "I don't think so. They had a few bad years not long after Anna was born, but they worked through it and became closer than ever. I don't think Carl would hide anything from Maria. He knew she shared the combination with me. He might not would have done the same, but he understood that I was her backup, and would always be there for Anna if anything happened to them. He knew."

"Okay, so tomorrow, when James and I go to Utley to gather the girls, you need to come and, in the presence of some disinterested party, open the safe."

"Who is the disinterested party?" Maggie enquires. "Might I suggest, me?"

"Way ahead of you there. Two cars? You ladies go up tonight and we follow tomorrow?"

She nods consent. "How about sending that lawyer of Miquel's. Shoot, I forgot the two imposters are still there."

Sylie responds in an almost lifeless voice. "That is easy. Call ahead and ask for them to be put in the guest house, which is where I lived, for the night. Then when we go up, we," she indicates herself and Maggie, "will go straight to that house and stay. There are lots of places to hide people on that estate."

"Okay, we are getting somewhere, what about Amur? Sylvie, do you know him?" Maggie looks over, she indicates that she doesn't. Rodger looks at the two of them.

"He seems to have been a really good friend of Carl's. I have some pictures of them together in Indonesia, we think, at a party. Could I ask you to take a close look to make sure you aren't familiar with him?"

Both ladies seem more curious than concerned. He drags out his briefcase, gets the file on Amur and shows the pictures to them. At first they are looking primarily at the men. Carl they both know, Amur, Maggie knows, and then they expand their perusal and notice the woman. Maggie's eyes narrow, Sylvie gasps. "She resembles Naydar"

"Can't be, she is too old. See how young Carl appears? Who is she?" Maggie says.

"Not anyone I have ever known, but yes, her resemblance to Naydar is something James and I noticed. "

He grabs his phone, that ever present phone, and begins to set in motion the trips for tonight and tomorrow. James will get their trip together while good ole Dave gets the honor of driving the ladies up tonight. It is time to review what comes next and in what order the pieces must fall. He reflects that timetables would work perfectly if people were not involved.

Chapter 27

The drive from the city to Utley takes the ladies through a conversation about the basic greed of people and the enormous task of finding, assembling, vetting, and getting approval for every piece of paper needed to prove first that Anna is Anna, and second, that she is the legal heir to Benson Enterprises. By the time Dave throws in a few remarks everyone in the car is feeling a bit more kindly toward the much maligned COO of Benson Enterprises.

Maggie has all her belongings in the car with no idea what comes next after the gathering of the girls. Sylvie is a bit better off, knowing where she will be staying. The one with no idea of where his next stop will be is Dave. He might stay at Utley for a while, he might get to fly the imposters out, or he might just turn around and drive Maggie back to the city. Right now, he considers himself lucky to know where he will sleep tonight. If he had his choice, he would head to a Caribbean Island tomorrow and spend the next few weeks basking in the sun. Somehow, he assumes he will not be asked.

As they pull through the gate, the bored news media try to halt the car to find out 1) who is in it, and 2) what they might be doing here this late at night. Maggie tells them her name and that she treated Anna during the tsunami. With that much information, they must be satisfied. No one gets a good glimpse at Sylvie who hunches back into the seat, her scarf covering part of her face.

Dave follows Sylvie's directions and drives around the back of the main house pulling up to to the guest house before discharging his passengers. The ladies go inside while Dave heads back up the drive to the garage and from there into the main part of the estate. He is met by an ecstatic Phil who is so tired of feminine company that he might re-enlist in the service.

In the main living area, they are greeted by Anna, Naydar, and the housekeeper. Dave goes through the plans for tomorrow with the group there, while Maggie takes that role in the guest house with the two actresses. She tells them to stay away from windows and doors for today and part of tomorrow and promises their release from this charade is almost over. They have been intrigued and well paid, but the bit is getting old and they are ready for new adventures and new challenges.

It is morning before Maggie and Sylvie make their way to the main house. There they are greeted enthusiastically by *their* girls. Everyone sits down to breakfast. "Who is feeding the others?" asks Naydar.

"There is a cook there and a kitchen," Sylvie smiles. She has grown rather fond of the Indonesian teen. "They will be fine."

Phil is looking forward to leaving as much as the guests. He is not used to staying put this long at one place. He is smiling and talking more than Anna remembers. The group at the guest house is staying out of sight, but Sylvie returns to watch over them. The morning passes. Everyone pretends to be involved in something, but truth be told, they are all in waiting mode. Phil and Dave talked late into the night and the fatigue shows in his lack of answers.

Anna really wants to be with Sylvie but at the same time, she doesn't wish to hurt Maggie's feelings. So all day the group pretends to pay attention to each other while every ear strains toward the sound of motors. Not long after they all pretend to lunch, the welcome sounds are heard. Naydar runs to the window and stands there looking down the long drive. The photographers at the gate have their cameras poised. There is a cheer from the group when Anna steps up beside her friend and the cameras click away. The cars pause briefly at the gate, giving those gathered there a good look at who is inside. Rodger speaks to them for a moment, then the procession heads toward the door. When Anna turns around, Sylvie is standing in the back doorway smiling at her. There is an atmosphere of renewal in the room.

The door opens and the group enters with the exception of the four security people who remain with the cars. Rodger steps in first. The girls run to him, hugging him, while James ushers in Mr. Shelbee. Introductions follow. Mr. Shelbee appears suspicious of everyone, but he is put at ease by Anna who slides effortlessly into the role of hostess, one that she has been grooming for since childhood. When everyone is seated and hot d'oeuvres have been served, she points the conversation to him.

"We are most glad to have you here today, Mr. Shelbee, was it? But I admit I am a bit confused as to your purpose?"

He places his cup on the table, looks at her and says, "I represent your husband."

Rodger and James begin to protest, but Anna stops them with a wave of her hand. "I am afraid it is you that is confused. I'm not married." her voice firm but soft. "I recently graduated from school and was to begin my higher education, but... " she looks down, Naydar glares at the lawyer.

"It is my understanding," he responds his voice louder and much less kind, "you married my client a day before the storm. I also understand that your memory is not sound, and my client wishes to take his proper place as your spouse and your protector."

"And who might your client be?" she asks.

Rodger squirms, but James is watching her face and he motions Rodger to be still.

"My client is Michael Gilbeck,"

Anna turns toward Sylvie in confusion, "I met a young man named Michael at the beach. I think it was the day before the storm. He and I talked, we met the next day, and decided to walk all the way to the water, which due to the tide was quite far out. As a matter of fact, we were discussing the unusual depth of the beach when the wave first became noticeable. Sorry, I don't know what happened to Michael. The last I saw, he was holding on to a ... a boat I think. I went under and that is the last I remember until the hospital. I think I might have commented on his last name. Are you kin to this man, Sylvie?"

Mr. Shelbee looks over at the nanny. This isn't where he expected this conversation to go. He has no plan for the next statement.

"I am not sure, dumpling," begins Sylvie as she crosses the room to sit next to Anna, "He might be a cousin."

"Oh, of you and Mom?" Anna's question has thrown Mr. Shelbee into utter silence.

"There was a cousin who lived in Germany. He had a son named Michael. What a wonder it would be if this is him." She turns toward the lawyer. "You say he claims to have married Anna? Does he say that they eloped? For you must understand, her mother would never have agreed to a marriage with such close ties."

Mr. Shelbee clears his throat. "My client really needs to come here to the states to clear this up. He contacted me through a legal office in Australia. I understand there are some transcripts of his statements in the hospital records?" He turns toward Maggie with the question hanging in the air.

She smiles unflustered. "I do believe he said something of the sort a few days after he arrived in triage. You might check with the nurse in charge of recording utterances from patients. She might have a record."

"Did the two have contact while in your care?" The question is out there; the tone is sharp.

"No, I'd have to check for dates, but my recollection is that he came in the day she was discharged to Jakarta."

"But he knows your name and something about your situation?" this goes toward Anna.

"I told you, I remember meeting him the day before the storm. We talked. I can't remember every detail of what was said, but I think I'd remember if I married a stranger on a beach right before being swept out to sea." Anna's tone reveals her irritation. Sylvie pats her hand.

"And you madam," he directs his attention to Sylvie, "Have you ever met the gentleman? You say he might be kin to you, but do you know?"

"No."

"I am puzzled, Mr. Stanton, did you bring me here to talk me out of this lawsuit, or is there another purpose?"

"Both," replies James. "I think you see the suit will be challenged. I'd advise you to be careful not to put too many man hours or financial assets into it, but that is my opinion and it is free of charge. While you are here we would like you, as an impartial officer of the court, to witness the opening of the safe here and the recording of any and all documents."

"You will need two witnesses. This hasn't already been done?"

"No, Anna has been here while we were attempting to sort company business from estate matters. When you wanted to talk with her, we considered that might be a good time to ferret out the estate papers."

"I will examine the papers?"

"If you wish. We have nothing to hide."

He turns to Anna, "Would you lead the way, my dear?"

She rises and, with Sylvie close by her side, heads to her father's office. Her face is white, her lips set. "I haven't been in here yet, this was Dad's place. His presence… it is as if I can still smell him. He would work there, and I played here at his feet."

"Where is the safe?" asks Mr. Shelbee as he looks about. Anna smiles, walks to a huge picture of her as a child out in the garden along with her dog. She touches the dog and the picture swings aside to reveal a wall safe. She stops, turns, shrugs. "I don't know the combination."

Before anyone can speak, Mr. Shelbee looks at James, "Surely you have the combination."

"Nope. Anna did your parents ever tell you of anyone who has that information?"

"Well, no, but if mom knew, then Sylvie would know," she beamed and glanced at the nanny standing right behind her father's desk. "Do you?"

Sylvie smiles at her and nods. She writes the combination on a piece of paper she pulls from the drawer, and hands it to Anna, who reads it, looks toward Sylvie, eyes radiant, turns back to the task at hand, and starts to open the safe.

"Wait," orders Mr. Shelbee. "We need a second impartial witness."

"I'm guessing that is what prompted my invitation to this gathering?" Maggie steps up beside the lawyer. "Proceed," she nods at the girl.

Anna returns her attention to the safe. Paper in hand not at eye level, she punches in a code, then twirls the dial, first left, then right, left once more. The click sounds out in the silence of the room as the door creaks open. The neat array of papers and official files are handed out one at a time to James with the two witnesses standing on each side as every piece of paper is documented. It is a long process. When everything is out of the safe, the two lawyers begin to sort them into business, personal, and estate stacks. Anna sits with Naydar and Sylvie going through an album full of pictures from her childhood.

"We have to get back to the office in New York to examine these in a better environment," says James. Rodger nods his agreement, suggests that they all head back to the city. Mr. Shelbee concurs.

Rodger confers with Phil leaving his instructions for the remainder of the day plus tomorrow's assignment. Then he rounds up the two girls, while James, with Maggie and Mr. Sheblee watching, carefully packages the material.

The first car transporting the girls heads out as Maggie retrieves her suitcase. They are stopped at the gate by enquiring media as he had assumed. A short time passes and they climb back into the vehicle heading toward the city. The news reporters with their cameras follow, allowing the second car with James, Mr. Shelbee, Maggie and the contents of Carl and Maria Benson's safe to pass with little to no scrutiny.

Chapter 28

It is Saturday now, and everything is running far more smoothly than anyone would have thought possible two days ago. Anna and Naydar are safely back in the penthouse with Ellen Hale watching over them. Maggie is ensconced in the guest quarters. With the girls back in the city all media leaves the area surrounding the estate, so Dave and Phil are on their way to the Caribbean with two chores. First they will drop the actresses at a plush resort for the week, provided that they sign the non-disclosure clause that remains in effect for five years. If they choose to continue the clause, they will receive extra bonus pay. From here the guys will pick up the nurse and fly her to her new position with a wealthy family in Brazil. Sylvie is left alone at the estate to manage any questions or enquires that might arise.

The schedule is set for the week. Amur is to come in on Monday. Then Tuesday will be the day for Anna's appointment with Dr. Walker. Wednesday becomes the "catch anything we are missing" day. The briefing on the situation with the estate is set to happen on Thursday. Meanwhile, James and his best legal department employees are hard at work going through every paper pertaining to Carl and Maria's wills and anything that might relate to the estate. Rodger is shifting through every scrap concerning Benson Enterprises and the way going forward. In other words, everyone is straining to have all in place by Thursday.

Amur calls in to say he is in the city and would like to talk with Rodger before the Monday's meeting which he rightly assumes will be like a deposition. Rodger agrees as long as James is present. And now they wait, making small talk, for the allotted time. "Have you found the will yet?" He asks.

"Yes, it is very involved. I am thinking there might be another out there somewhere. We have yet to get the court order to check the safety deposit box at Carl's bank. This one is almost word for word what I executed for him years ago, but it does contain an interesting change. It leaves the business and properties to Maria, should she survive, and to any children."

"Okay, that sounds reasonable. What has changed?"

"The original said Maria and Annalisel."

"So maybe he planned on more babies."

"Maybe, but this copy is dated fourteen months ago. I wasn't asked to cowrite or witness it. Seems strange to me."

Rodger shrugs. His mind is racing concerning not only the will but the business. "Does it mention any age limit for Anna taking on the directorship of Benson Enterprises?"

James scans the pages as if he hasn't looked for that or needs to review it. "Well, in this section, it does suggest that if Anna is the sole heir before her twenty first birthday that she have a court appointed guardian and a receivership be appointed to run the company until such time as she achieves her majority. You and I would be the receivership."

"Why did he not tell us, at least you, this? You are the head of his legal department as well as his friend."

"And he trusted you to run this company with little help from him for years. You are asking something that I have no answers for."

There is a call from the front desk that Amur is on his way up. The two look at each other. "Wonder if he has any answers," muses Rodger.

A knock on the door announces the arrival of their guest.

"Enter."

Amur walks confidently into the office and shakes hands, "Hello, how are you doing? Everything going well?" he questions.

"Pretty much," Rodger says, "But we do have a few questions. How about you? All well with you? Did you suffer any damage from the storm?"

"Personally no, but my family yes. My sister and her child lived in the path of the wave. I'm sorry to report she didn't make it. She died the same day as the Bensons."

"You never told me."

"You never asked until now."

Rodger looks down, James clears his throat and pats Amur's shoulder. "Sorry man, we were caught up in the business and didn't think."

"I understand, each takes care of his own, right? My first thought when you sent me to Benkulu was Carl because of the job. I actually didn't realize my sister had moved there until I was there looking for the Bensons. What is, is. We move ahead. Now, what is the purpose for which I am needed Monday?"

"We need to go over any and all that you did to secure Anna's identification, and I am a bit curious about you and Carl's relationship."

Amur raises his dark, swarthy eyebrows as if surprised. "Mr. Benson and me?"

"Yes, I have copies of pictures of the two of you in what appears to be a social setting. Were you more than an employee?"

"You know how we met?"

No reaction.

"We met in Iraq before Carl's business was up and going. He was there at the behest of the American government, and I was assigned to watch over him. I spoke the language. He was kidnapped. I retrieved him. After his business began making money, he hired me to look after the ventures in the Mid East. We have been friends, companions, and business associates for years."

"Why... "

"Did he not tell you of our association? I cannot answer. Maybe he thought to keep New York separate from Indonesia. I do not know. How did he leave the company? Do I still have a position? Do I report to you?" This question is leveled directly at Rodger, who wonders at its foundation.

"We are trying to get all our paperwork and legal matters in line, so we can find out if any of us have a job. If we cannot prove Anna to be the legal heir, the company will be sold at auction and the proceeds will go to Carl's five favorite charities," James informs him.

"Just Anna? No other heirs?"

"Not that we are aware of. There is a challenge to the will from a young man who claims to be Anna's husband. I think we can handle that now that Anna has regained her memory."

"All of her memory?"

"Well, she is due at the doctor's office Tuesday and I think we will let her make that determination." Rodger is super still and hyper watchful. James watches the two. It is as if they are two warring dogs circling each other. The room is charged with testosterone.

"Is there something else we might need to know here?" asks James.

"Did he tell you he ask me to make sure DNA would declare Anna the daughter of Carl Benson?"

"What?" Rodger explodes. "You said something about working the identification backward, and that I didn't want to know what you were going to do. How can you now say I did know?"

"Because you are not a stupid man, Mr. Madden. You knew very well what I meant, and it would be in your best interest to keep me well out of your little proceedings. That is if you are as smart as I think you are."

"And what exactly did you do?" James asks.

Amur looks at Rodger, again the bushy eyebrows raise as if to question his desire to have the information outed. Silence descends. Rodger asks James if he would leave for a few moments. "It might be better if Amur and I continue without Benson legal counsel at this point."

James nods and exits the room.

"Okay, now what is it that you need to tell me?"

"By the way are you certain that the girl is Annalisel Benson? You need to be aware that there might be a glitch that rose to the surface because of the attempt to make the DNA match. "

"Yes, her memories of her childhood have returned, the places and things from her home. Her nanny also identifies her. She is Anna."

"You don't really need me to provide the DNA test then?"

"No"

"Then what it the problem? Why did you call me in?"

"One was to find out about your connection to Carl. The second to ask you about some pictures of you and your date with Carl at some social gathering? Your date looks a lot like Naydar."

"My date? Oh yes, my date, that is Naydar's mother."

"Oh, well, I think you are right in thinking that we need to leave you out of this unless the court requires your presence. However, until we have everything established, i's dotted, t's crossed, I'd like you to remain in New York."

"Fine, I will be at the Waldorf, but on company billing of course." There it is the smile. The old Amur backs back, the man he knew in Indonesia. So why does Rodger have a sick feeling in the pit of his stomach that tells him he there is much he hasn't heard.

Amur leaves, he and James discuss the visit briefly, and then James leaves headed to Claire while Rodger is back to downing acid reflux controllers and wondering how so many things could change in such a small amount of time. Sunday, the free day, the day to relax, is now the what next day.

Chapter 29

Sunday starts so quietly, Rodger is almost tempted to flee the city before any one realizes he is awake, but, he decides, that is the action of a coward. He gathers his thoughts and heads to the penthouse to share brunch with the ladies. The door opens to laughter. Good Lord, he needs this. The group is secure, they are sharing ideas and silly memories from this their common adventure. They dwell on the ridiculous as opposed to the catastrophic, and he listens, smiles when they paint him as the butt of a joke, as layer after layer of stress drip from his conscious until it seems time has melted away, he feels lighter, less suspicious, more himself.

His gaze rests on Naydar. He sees her smiles, watches her reach toward Anna when something grabs her attention, observes the sideways glances in Maggie's direction and he wonders yet again of her parentage. Amur, is he the father of this darling sprite? Dark, swarthy Amur? Surely not. She is delicate, light skinned, a lovely child. He wonders how old is she? He wonders why he has never asked.

He catches Maggie's attention and motions toward the kitchen. The cook is putting the finishing touches on brunch. He continues to the balcony with a puzzled Maggie trailing him. Once the door is closed, he looks out over the street and says, "Do you know how old Naydar is?"

"No, is there a problem?"

"Just curious. How would you compare her age and Anna's?"

"Okay, now you have my attention, why do you want to know?"

"The two of them have quite a connection don't you think?"

Her hand grazes his arm, " Short term intensity will create fierce relationships. You, yourself, grew close to Bobby, Evelyn, and even me. We would not have captured your attention except for the extreme circumstances, would we?"

He shakes his head, "No, probably not, not the same circles," he admits. "Something, it is nothing definite, but something nags at me. Wish I could ask her about her background without disturbing her."

"Is Amur in town yet? Ask him to talk with her."

"No, I think we will muddle through without involving him. Do you think she looks like anyone you know?"

"Now you really have me wondering. What brought all this up?"

"Doctor Maggie, Mr. Rodger, our meal is prepared. Come on, we are hungry," Naydar herself has come to bring them in.

"Coming," Maggie beams as Rodger extends his arm and escorts her to the table.

Two hours later, Rodger is back at his apartment, his empty apartment. Gone is the laughter, the jokes, the joy. He turns on the television. He watches without seeing the news of the day. Someone is threatening someone, someone is belittling someone. Somehow, it never changes. His thoughts run like a tape on a wheel. He retraces all the steps he has taken since James popped into his office announcing the storm and its possible affect on the lives of those in his circle, in his business, those about whom he now feels responsible. Damn, he does feel responsible. When did that happen? The realization shocks him out of his stupor. He makes his way to the room where all the investigative files lay. He picks up the files of Carl, Maria, and Amur. It is the latter to which he turns first. Once more the pictures draw him. Again he picks out the two of the party. He reaches for a magnifying glass. It is the woman he focuses on. He scans the picture into his computer, reworks it to isolate the woman, enlarges it, and prints it. It is Naydar's spitting image.

The next action is to contact Curtis Walden, the detective. Fortunately, he is free and one hour later is in Rodger's apartment discussing the files. Rodger questions him about how he gathered the information, if he had asked about the woman in the picture, or the occasion. Walden begins to explain his procedures, he focuses on the person who is the subject of the file, not anything or anyone else.

"So, you don't know who this woman is?"

"No sir, I don't. I do believe those pictures were in both Mr. Saluar and Mr. Benson's files. Would you like us to continue with the investigation and attempt to the identify the woman?"

"Yes, and especially any and all connections to either gentleman. I'd also like to know where she is now and what she does." He walks toward the door and opens it.

The detective deduces that the conference is over. He rises, gathers his materials and starts to leave.

"I need the information as soon as possible," Rodger has already dismissed the conversation and is back to rereading the file. He reads everything they have on Amur. If he divides it into pre Carl information and post Carl information, the distinction is alarming. There is one brief paragraph pertaining to his life before he and Carl became friends. It has his place of birth and his connection with the Indonesian government. The last sentence is his hiring on with a private security company operating in the Middle East. He is fluent in five languages. His resume is perfect for the job he was hired to do.

After his rescue of Carl Benson, he never returns to the private company, instead, he is hired by Carl as his head of security in the area. He has proved to be a reliable employee, and the hire has benefitted both parties. According to the file, Amur has never married. His personal life is private, little is known. Rodger sits with the file in his hands and wonders. He is determined to know as much as possible before his next encounter with his enigmatic employee. He wonders what is going on now. What does a man with little past, except for that which is work related, do alone in New York City. He reaches for his phone. Another agent is put on the case before Curtis Walden returns to his office.

Rodger's next call is to James. He catches him up on the happenings of the day as to his request for more information on the elusive Mr. Saluar. James agrees they need more information then asks if another interview with Amur has been scheduled. "Not yet," is the terse answer. Thursday's proceedings loom large.

James has news also. "Mr. Shelbee has called and Michael is in the city demanding an audience with Anna."

Rodger shakes his head and sighs. "Stall until after Tuesday and we will see where we are then."

"Are the merger papers up to date?" James asks breaking the thought cycle.

"Next on the agenda, next." he looks over at the table that holds that paperwork and sighs again, "Next," he mumbles as he ends the conversation and picks up the merger file.

Chapter 30

Monday morning brings its own share of surprises. The first appears on the ring finger of Claire Daily's left hand. She makes sure he notices by putting that hand forward with every word. She does everything but pull the "is it hot in here to you?" stunt. He grins but plays at ignoring her until she pushes her hand in his face. "I'm engaged," she says.

"Great, who to?" he mocks.

She pushes him away. "Silly," she returns to her desk and sits admiring her jewelry. James walks in wearing a sheepish grin, glances in his direction, then blows a kiss to his fiancée. Rodger punches his shoulder, congratulates them both and ushers James into his office. The two men stare at each other grinning. Then the work day begins.

First they go over the legalities in the proposed merger contract. Rodger is impatient with what he considers extreme caution on the part of the potential partner. "It is as if they are deliberately stalling on every count. There is a vetting of each word."

"I think I understand where this is originating," says James. "They know there is a court hearing coming on the estate, and they might have guessed that there is a potential question concerning the stability of the company. I'd advise caution if I were their legal council."

"But you aren't, you are ours. We must find a way to separate the business matters from the estate or get this estate filing done as soon as possible."

"That is what we are trying to do." James flops into the chair. "We can't go any faster unless you want to go without the medical depositions."

"Speaking of medical disposition," he began when the buzzer on his desk went off.

"Mr. Madden, there is a young man on his way up. We tried to stop him here, but he charged into an open elevator and is headed your way. I have a security detail coming but I don't know that they will get there before he does. Sir, Should I call NYPD? "

"No, not yet. Tell me what you observed about him."

"He is tall, very pale, looks as if he might be sick, or maybe mental. He was sputtering in English and another language which I do not know. His face makes me think he has been in a really bad fight sometime ago, and hasn't yet healed. He is pissed, Boss. Majorly pissed."

At this point, the bell announcing the elevator sounds and James heads out to confront the newcomer, while Rodger finishes the conversation, then comes forward also. There in Claire Dailey's area and in her face is the man in question. He is tall, and pale, but the most obvious part of the description is that he is definitely angry. He is pushing at James trying to bypass him on his way to the office. Rodger stand in the doorway, stares at the youngster, and in a stern voice asks, "Who are you, and what are you doing here?"

"I am Michael Gilbeck, and I have come here to find out where my wife is, and why you are keeping me from seeing her."

"Well, Mr. Gilbeck, should you wish to make an appointment with my secretary, I will try to take these questions under consideration. However, I would suggest you bring your lawyer to the conference."

"You Bastard, you know I have no lawyer. He dropped my case after he talked to you." The words erupted from his mouth with such force that they bring out spittle. "I want answers and I want them now." he shouts as the stairway door opens and four uniformed security guards burst into the tension.

Rodger lifts his hand to indicate they should stand back. "Well, Mr. Gilbeck, that isn't going to happen. Again, if you wish to make an appointment, Ms. Dailey will fit you into the schedule. I think there is an opening tomorrow afternoon. Ms. Dailey, can you check that out?"

Claire pretends to examine the book at her desk. "Yes sir, There is a break at 3:30 tomorrow. It is a half hour slot."

James is still keeping himself between the intruder and his fiancee. "I'd advise you to take it and leave now," he says.

Michael stops pushing, glares around at the crowd that now surrounds him, and sputters something under his breath in German. Claire holds out an appointment reminder card which Michael snatches as he turns toward the elevator. The security contingent boards with him. The door closes to three relieved people. Claire's hands are shaking as James grasps them. Rodger slumps against the office door, looks at them, shakes his head, and mutters something about another fire to put out.

Fifteen minutes later when James walks in to the office, he finds his friend on the phone with security scheduling a pick up of Sylvie from the estate to end at Claire's apartment. "At this rate, we might need to sublet your fiancee's place," he mockingly quips as he checks out the usually solid head of legal. He appears to be calmer and almost normal. " Ask Claire to call the good Dr. Walker and see, if as an emergency, could she spare us the whole day tomorrow. I have a feeling we are going to need it."

As he is talking James' phone rings. The conversation is short and to the point. He hangs up and says, "The court has appointed you and me co- executors of Carl and Maria's estate, and as such we have access to any and all lock boxes. I'll go and gather all the paperwork, and then, do you want to accompany me to the two banks?"

"No, you go ahead, I think it might be best if one of us stayed here. Things are getting a little crazy, and I do think you, as the lawyer, should be the one to delve into the boxes. You will know what we need and what we don't. Do you want a security detail with you?"

"Yesterday, I would have laughed at that," James begins.

From the doorway, Claire looks up at Rodger, "Please."

He nods starts toward the office, stops, and says, "Anyone comes up that elevator, I want to know. I don't care what floor they ask for, and Claire, if that elevator rings, I want you inside my office. Understood?"

"Yes sir, Thank you."

James glances his thanks. Rodger retreats to give them a bit of time. As he does, he remembers to call Sylvie to catch her up on the day's action. She is perplexed but states her willingness to come with the team. He sits down, considers what happened, and breathes. His buzzer rings again, this time the person asking for permission to come up is Amur. This isn't the time, but Rodger is wanting answers. He asks if Amur could come back at five. He listens as the desk manager repeats the question. The answer is yes. He calls Claire to put it on her calendar, puts it on his and then, on the spur of the moment calls Curtis Welden. No progress has been made on the identity of the mystery woman from the photos. But there is news. Amur has been in the city for ten days.

"Where?"

"Don't know yet Boss, still tracing his movements. Want I should call you if we find anything?"

"And if you don't. I want to hear either way before five."

"Rodger, Boss." The call is dropped, and he wanders to Claire's area.

"I want no calls through to me unless it is Welden, James, Sylvie, or Amur canceling his appointment. Phone the penthouse and inquire as to how everything is going there. Tell Maggie what has happened here and for her to be on alert. Check that, beef up the security detail at the penthouse. Oh, and are you okay?"

She smiles, "Yes, I am fine. How about you?"

"We make it through this mess, and I promise. Then vacations for everyone. How does that sound?"

Claire's laughter follows him back into the office. He marshals his thoughts, trying to put some kind of order to the chaos that has been his morning. He has until five to figure things out.

Chapter 31

First of all, he has to focus on Amur and the conversation that will be today. Tomorrow will have to wait until, well, tomorrow. He picks up the now worn file with Amur's name on it and begins to leaf through. As he reads, he jogs down questions he wants answered. Family? The woman in the photo? What does Amur know about Naydar's family? What is the glitch on the DNA? What he has been doing in the city for the last two weeks?

It is as if each question brings another to the surface. The more he concentrates on what he knows, the surer he is that there is way more he doesn't know. He remembers discussions with others about Amur and how several had trust issues with the man. He remembers Bobby expressing some misgivings, and also Maggie saying that he, Amur, had shown her pictures of Naydar's mother. He stops, Naydar's mother?

He phones the penthouse. The housekeeper answers. Rodger asks if she has the number to the fax machine in his office. Puzzled she searches and replies in the positive. He asks her to get Maggie and have her fax the picture of Naydar's mother to his office.

Five long minutes stretch out like hours. Then he hears the welcome chatter of the fax. There appears a dated photograph. Rodger picks it out and compares it to the blown up picture of Amur's "date". It is the same woman, without question. So that question answered. Now to what her relationship is to him. That is not so obvious. Rodger looks again at his list of questions, and back to the file. According to the file, he has a sister…, did Phil say she was talking on the phone to an uncle? Could this be the connection? The more he ponders the possibles, the more this one stands out. It is Amur who led him to Naydar; he could have set her up with Carl and Maria in like fashion.

It is three, He has eaten nothing since breakfast. He pushes the intercom button and asks Claire Dailey to step in. She walks in with her tablet ready for notes. He smiles and asks, "Had any lunch?"

"No," she glances at the watch on her wrist, "Good grief, it is almost quitting time."

"I'll let you leave early if you will go get me something to eat, I am starved."

She smiles, raises her eyebrows in inquiry. He shrugs. Another smile and she is gone. In half an hour she is back with a salad, a steak sandwich, chips, and a slice of pie. There is coffee in a cup from the coffee shop in the lobby. Rodger, rubs his hands in anticipation, "You can go now if you want, I am a happy man."

"You are easy to please, sure you don't need me to stay until your meeting?"

"No, I'd rather be alone for that, and you will serve the company better by going to your apartment and making sure everything is in place for Ms. Gilbeck. Then, if you would, talk with her about her expectations for tomorrow's confrontation. Gently lead her to confide as much as she knows about the people who raised this young man, and what sort of ideas they might have instilled in him. I am not wanting to be blindsided again. Think you can do that? Oh, by the way, James wasn't planning on coming back here was he?"

"I'm not sure, but he didn't say anything to me about waiting on him. Do you think I should call?"

Rodger pauses, "Yes, I think that would be great. Then maybe he could come to your place tonight, you could both talk with Sylvie and then maybe leave her and celebrate your engagement?"

Claire's smile is a face buster. "Thanks, Boss. You know, you're not such a cold-hearted, evil man after all."

His head jerks up in surprise as her laughter follows her out the door. Soon he hears the opening of the elevator and is now alone with his late lunch and his thoughts. The dossier and his notes are on his desk, he sits at the small table in the conference area and looks around his space as if seeing it, truly seeing it for the first time. HIs office is a large room subdivided by working spaces. His huge desk is prominent, occupying the direct path between the door to the reception area and the bank of windows that form its backdrop. On one side of the desk is every kind of electronic machine needed to gather and disseminate information in the fast moving world of modern business. Some of the electronics are built into the desk, giving him access to information unnoticeable to anyone else standing in the office. Other devices stand up and are available to share information with business associates. One side of the desk is open to the room, the other is closed.

Against the wall to the open side of his desk are several cabinets with document files that he uses when necessary. Beyond them is a bookcase loaded with books on energy in various forms. Where he sits now there is a couch that has served as bed many times, three chairs and a round table that he uses to serve tea, or coffee to clients. It is an extremely, attractive place, very masculine in tone and furnishings. As he chews, he looks around at the tasteful art that fills the wall space. The value of the paintings alone would keep that make shift clinic in Benkulu afloat for years. Startled at the thought that evades his brain, he considers this space and remembers the areas of Indonesia that he traveled through and the sites that withstood the disaster. Good Lord, you could house three families in this office alone, and how many offices, albeit not this size, were in this building? One building, he shakes his head.

He must stop these memories and focus. Amur will be here soon, and he must, no, will be ready. Rodger calms his mind as he stuffs away the remnants of his meal. He steps into the private bathroom which has its own shower. He cleans up, checking out his grooming, and putting back on his suit jacket. He is the titular head of Benson Enterprises, at least until Thursday and he must portray that position. He puts away all personal files in the proper cabinet, tidies up the sitting area and types all the questions he wishes answered into the computer his visitor will not see. As an added precaution, he prepares the audio to record all conversation, not that he, Rodger, can't deal with Amur, but he might not remember his exact words and that could be important.

The clock hands move toward 4:30 and his finger tips began a steady beat on the desk. He is certain that Amur will be on time if not early. He needs the call from Curtis Welden now. Should he call? To display his anxiety is contrary to the appearance that he is working hard to achieve. He needs Amur to see him as the one in control. Call, damnit! Ten more minutes roll by before his private phone rings. Welden at last.

"Mr. Madden, I have a few notes for you. Number one, the lady in the picture is rumored to be the subject's sister, we are still following up on that. The sister did have a child, a girl, and her husband was killed in the boxing day tsunami, she was reported killed in this storm, quite an interesting coincidence. There is no report of the girl. He pauses as if checking his notes. Mr. Saluar has been in the city for ten days. In that time, he has met with a young lady in muslim head gear at the public library near the Benson penthouse at least once. The young lady seems to know him, however he appears to have initiated the meetings. He also spent time checking into the background of one of your other subjects, a Ms. Sylvie Gilbeck. He has requested many of the same documents we requested as we put together her folder. I doubt he has come across anything you do not have in her file. That is all we have."

"Thank you, Detective. I appreciate your efforts." The phone rests in his hands. The bell rings to signal the elevators arrival. It's time. He gathers himself, checks the computer, turns on the recorder.

Chapter 32

When he hears the knock on the door, he waits a full minute and a half before he calls, "Yes, come in."

The door opens to reveal Amur as expected. He is the same as usual, calm, dapperly dressed, alert, and confident. Rodger's head remains down watching the movement of a holding pattern on the computer screen. He motions for his guest to sit as he continues to look at nothing, then he raises his head, smiles, stands, and extends his hand. Amur purses his lips, grins, nods, and shakes the offered hand.

"Have a seat. It has been a bit crazy around here today." Rodger says as he reclaims his seat.

"I'll bet it has,"

Rodger wills himself not to frown. "So exactly what is it that you wish to discuss?"

"I want to talk with you about a few items," Amur begins, "I'm sure you agree we have a lot in common. Both of us have really good jobs that we love with a company that we hope continues to employ us. We both were friends of Carl Benson, and want his desires for the future of this company to come to fruition. This is why I come here today, there is information which has come into my hands that you and I need to discuss, and I am sure there is information that you have that we, together, need to hash out. You don't know me that well, so lets begin there. You ask whatever you feel you need to know about me and, if I agree that it is a need to know, I will answer. Of course I'll retain the right to do the same. Agreed?"

Rodger leans back in his chair, he watches Amur's face silently. "And anything said here will stay here? Truth only," he asks?"

Amur nods, "Handshake? Man's honor?"

Rodger inclines his head.

"Okay, you first Mr. Rodger Madden. Turn off the recorder and the computer. How did I know? Who did you think suggested and

The Wave Effect 167

purchased them for your office and for Carl's office. His are much the same except he has a camera in the wall that videos also."

Rodger tilts his head sideways. He reaches to the desk and pushes the button disengaging the computer after he stops the recorder. "And you," he asks, "Do you have a recording devise or camera?"

"Very good, you are learning." Amur places his phone on the desk face up to show it is turned off. he removes his coat and rolls up the sleeves. "I'm afraid that is as far as I am willing to go. You will have to take my word."

Rodgers presses his lips together, "Okay, tell me, Who is the woman in the pictures of you and Carl?"

"My sister, Naydar's mother. She was killed in the storm. We found the body the day after I first landed at Benkulu."

"That means Naydar is your niece, and you left her, your family, in that? Why? Why the big secret? Why not tell us?"

"I wasn't sure. I had never seen the child of my sister. She married without my family's approval, therefore she was shunned. I wondered when I saw her because she looked so much like Assandra, but then, I thought they lived in a small hill village. I intended to check her out after I got the Bensons off the Island. When I returned, I talked with her about her parents, she told me about her father's death and her mother's job at the hotel, and I accepted the relationship."

"Why didn't you take her out of there?"

Amur looks down at his fingers, "To what? I had no place to take her, and she seemed with all that was happening, to need to be needed. She didn't know me, she had never seen me. Anna Benson she knew and Anna needed her. She wanted to stay with Anna."

Again the circling goes around. "So your turn," Amur states. "Who is this Sylvie Gilbeck that serves as Anna's nanny?"

Rodger considers not answering, decides this is a test question. In all probability, the answer is to determine his intentions. An incorrect answer will terminate the discussion. In for a penny, in for a pound, he stares at his chief of Mid East Security, releases the tension in his shoulders, sighs, and says, "Maria Benson's cousin. They had a very close relationship as youngsters, or so I understand. And you, you are interested in this because..?" His hands splay outward, eyebrows lift.

"There is a boy, man, that we came across in the ward there in Benkulu. He said his name was Michael Gilbeck. He told me he had a relationship with Anna Benson and wanted to know if she were alive or dead. He seemed to feel he would be somehow involved in the company were she to have survived the storm. At our next meeting, he had learned of her amnesia, and at this time, he reported their marriage. Paperwork of any sort didn't survive the tsunami, I couldn't find anyway to prove or disprove his contention. The last I knew of him, he had been removed to Australia."

"Did you in anyway encourage him to come to the America, and discuss this?"

"I suggested that if he were serious about the allegations, he should have a lawyer, and it would be best if said lawyer was in the United States." He looks downward at his hands, "I surmise from your question, that he has a lawyer?"

"Had. The lawyer dropped him, at least that is what he says, when he, the lawyer, discovered Anna is alert, and that her memory has returned."

"So Anna has her memory back. All of it?"

"She is to be checked out by her psychiatrist tomorrow, but as far as we can tell her memory is stable, and her recollections of the time before the storm is accurate."

"Does she remember my sister at all?"

"Sorry, I knew nothing about your sister until today, so to my knowledge, no one has asked her about that. Didn't Naydar fill you in on her mother?"

"Yes, and no. She is the one that told me we needed to find her mother, but she didn't know what had happened to her, nor where she might be. When we found her body, it was already at the airport, I wasn't told where she was found. Probably, near the hotel, she worked there."

"How did Naydar find a job working as a maid in the hotel, and how did she happen to be assigned to the Bensons?"

Amur shrugs his shoulders, "She could have arranged that."

"Your sister?"

He nods. "Your turn, How did Michael happen upon the Bensons, not sure I can handle that degree of coincidence."

Both men shake their heads and frown in unison each watching the other. "Yes, that would be beyond incredulousness."

"Do you intend to question Michael?" He is watching Rodger's eyes, body stance, his hands. Very observant is the visitor.

"Yes, I have a meeting scheduled for tomorrow at 3:30," is the terse reply.

"Might I sit in?"

Now it is Rodger who is watching for any slight reaction. "I think not. The meeting needs to stay as calm as possible."

"I am and have been your security advisor for the whole Mid Eastern region for years. I had Carl's complete trust. I need yours; but you also need mine. There is something going here that, in my opinion, neither of us has a grip on yet. We must work together or we could lose everything."

"You ask me to trust you, to include you, yet, I am not privy to the supposed glitch in the DNA? You need to know what is going on with Michael, I need to know what is going on with you. Trust has to be mutual."

Amur stares, then nods and shifts forward in his chair. "If I confide in you, you must allow me to be part of the decision as to what comes next."

"And James? Will he be a part of our coterie?"

"You want him in?"

"Yes, I think I must insist that he be a part of this."

"Is he available now, or do you wish to continue this discussion later? It needs to happen sometime before the settlement of the estate. I assure you it will be in your best interest."

"The glitch?"

Amur's nod is all Rodger's stomach needs to go on permanent maneuvers. He takes out his private phone and calls James who answers before Rodger has time to focus. "Is there any way possible that you can drop by here like now?"

James doesn't push back as expected, "On my way, give me five."

Rodger blinks, he must have been headed here without the call. Stomach rolls yet again. The two in the office are silent. Talking seems to be pointless as they wait. This is going to be a three way decision.

Chapter 33

James doesn't bother to knock. He has his briefcase, and a couple of folders in his hands as he enters the room. His glance tells Rodger that he expected to see Amur there. He extends his hand as he is introduced. The two men have talked by phone many times, but this is their first face to face meeting. "I have been in touch with Ms. Dailey, she made me aware of this meeting, and I think I can guess the purpose, sort of a fill in the blanks all around?"

Rodger nods. Amur extends his hand. "We have been going over what we think we need to share in order to make Thursday's court proceedings reflect what is our vision for the company."

James raises an eyebrow and waits.

"I think time would be best served if you brought Mr. Stanton up to date on our discussions. I will reserve the right to add anything I feel needs to be included," says Amur.

Rodger repeats the gist of the conversation between himself and Amur, then turns to him and asks, "Anything I left out?"

Amur indicates he is fine with the material shared. Then adds that they, the three of them, need to prepare the way forward for the sake of the company.

"Yes, I would agree with you," says James, "And I am looking forward to working with you. Can you tell us what the DNA glitch is?"

Rodger fights hard not to let his amazement of the ease with which James is accepting the new threesome. Meanwhile, Amur settles back down in his chair. "I was most anxious to prove that the girl in the clinic was Anna, that I decided to take DNA samples from our patient and place part of them in spaces that she had previously lived."

Rodger mutters, "DNA backward."

"Precisely," Amur agrees. "So I asked Naydar to gather some drippings from her mouth as well as some hair to take for testing."

James holds up his hand. "Didn't Naydar tell you it was Anna?"

"Yes, but I wanted other proof. She had also been through the storm, and we had just viewed the broken body of her mother. I wasn't sure she was a great witness. So I brought the hair and spittle to New York. Here I pretended to check out the penthouse for "samples". I was going to also take some hair to Switzerland to her school. But first, I decided to have it tested, curiosity won out. When I took it to a lab that I have used many times before, they told me we had an interesting problem. There where two different samples of hair with similar, but not exact DNA. The samples were from two different individuals, but the two were related." Here he stops in his narrative to allow his two listeners to catch up. The jerk of the heads and the stare of both men leads him to his next point.

"The strands of hair are from biological siblings. Now, I didn't quite know what my next move needed to be. I never knew Maria well, and never knew Carl to be disloyal. I knew who had given me the brush, but.. " He stops looking at the other two.

James picks up the story. "The other sample is Naydar's correct?" He watches as Rodger's face goes from concerned to flabbergasted and Amur's from solemn to incredulous.

"Yes, how did… "

"That is why I was on my way here. In the lockbox of the bank, there were papers that show Carl was informed he had another daughter in January, 2004, the month after the Boxing day tsunami. A woman named…"

"Assandra," Amurs murmurs.

James holds out the file. "He makes a note here that he informed Maria and that they are both in agreement that his will should be changed to include this child. However, they want to become familiar with the girl before she is made aware of the connection. That is part of the reason for the vacation, and the reason Naydar was working for them at the hotel."

"I cannot believe that I did not guess. He and Assandra were friends. That I knew. He and Maria hit some sort of problem not long after Anna was born. That I also knew. I am a professional security person, but I never suspected." Amur is slumped in his chair his head going back and forth as he tries to assimilate the material. "Why did I not see this? She and that buffoon married so quickly after Carl and I left her in Jakarta. She should have told me."

"She didn't want you to know. So why does she tell him and why wait so long to do so?" Rodger comments.

James smiles the smile of a man familiar with love. "She didn't want to hurt him, but the tsunami of 04 killed her husband, drove her and her child to work in Benkulu. She didn't want that to be a forever situation for her girl. She must have been a special lady."

"She was," Amur answers, turning away from the others.

Rodger is silent. Ideas buzz through his head as he attempts to digest the conversation, and predict what it will mean to the next few days. "When do we tell Anna? She has this to absorb and the situation with Michael. Do we put it all on her at once?"

"I think we have to," James states. "The court proceedings are Thursday. She has to be prepared for whatever comes up and comes out. What about Naydar? Does she know, and if not do we tell her?"

"She doesn't know," Amur interjects, "and I prefer not to tell her until we see how Anna takes the news. She has been through so much already, and anything to spare her would be my preference."

"Agreed then, we will wait to tell Naydar, but we will tell Anna. Now what do we do about Michael?" James summarizes.

"Let me get first crack at Michael tomorrow, then we meet again after we see how that goes. And maybe we can find some firm ground between then and Thursday."

"I'd like to watch your meeting with Michael," Amur repeats, his voice indicating he is not prepared for a no.

"I'm beginning to think it might be best if both you watched it. Can you set that up?"

"Yes. Does anyone else need to be included?"

"I'd like to tell Claire, my fiancee, what is happening so she doesn't think I am dropping out on her, but she doesn't have to watch."

Rodger smiles; Amur frowns. "Amur, any objections to having Maggie or Anna's Psychiatrist watch the meeting if we can get them here?"

"Anyone else, like the third army battalion?"

"Nope, but maybe Anna should watch also. Otherwise, I think that covers it. We will meet at three and set up right?"

Amur stands. "2:30. The boy is anxious, he will be early."

Chapter 34

It is past seven when the meeting breaks up. Rodger is committed to escorting Anna and Maggie to Dr. Walker's office at nine thirty the next morning. He knows the hour is late, but he must make time tonight to check on and with Sylvie. Too much rests on her helping them deal with Michael. Before they leave the office, James calls Claire to let her know the two of them are bringing supper. They call ahead to a steak place that is on their way. The food is hot and ready when they arrive, and within the hour they are at Claire's apartment eating. The conversation is light and carried forward by the recently engaged couple. It is obvious Sylvie is uncomfortable, and Rodger is focused on something way beyond this shared meal. As soon as the dishes are taken into the kitchen, James and Claire excuse themselves leaving the other two watching each other.

Rodger clears his throat, and asks, "Did Claire bring you up to date on what is happening?"

"Yes," is the tense answer.

"Sylvie, I can only guess what you are experiencing. Here we have your child whom you have never known, and we are asking you to help us confront him. I do ask that you let me know if I am stepping too close to your personal territory."

She looks at him, head turned to the side, lips poked out, "Of course. What do you want to know?"

"You have never seen or heard from Michael?"

"Miguel, and the answer is not since the day of his birth."

"Okay, then what can you tell me about the people who adopted him. Did you know them?"

"Yes, but not well. They were cousins of my father. My father was a staunch German Christian conservative. He translated life by the rules he read in the old testament. I was to him an adulterer, therefore condemned. He might have stoned me if my mother had not intervened." She notices Rodger's face and the horror in his

The Wave Effect 177

expression. She chuckles, "Well, maybe not stoned, but he never allowed me to set foot in his house again. He kicked me out. I am sure the people he chose to take my baby were raised similarly to him. I was never shown affection from my father. He was head of the house and everyone else did his bidding. This will be the pattern that Miguel has seen modeled."

"And you? What happened to you?" The words are not unusual, but his tone is.

Sylvie stares, then continues in a broken monotone, "Maria is a new bride, she dares not ask her husband to move a relative into their home, but she sends me money to come to America and helps me until I find work. Swedes have a good reputation for the caring of children. I worked as a nanny for a family in New York for three years. Then Anna is born, and Maria calls me to become a nanny for her. Mrs. Benson the domineering mother-in-law, demands she hire someone. She pretends to be upset, but we are both delighted. I come to Utley and remain there, as Anna's nanny and Maria's friend. That old lady, she was... " Sylvie shakes her head, "difficult."

"I met her... once." The statement stands between them as a bond.

Sylvie smiles, "The rest is me and Anna, and Maria. Carl does not involve himself with the child until she charms him at the ripe old age of four. Then it is as if he cannot get enough of her. Me he never warms to, but Anna, she becomes his pride and joy. He goes from a man with no time for children to a doting father who is tickling strange little ones under the chin and handing out lollipops in the park. His business still requires him to spend long periods of time away from home, but now with me here, Maria accompanies him on many trips. On occasion, they will take Anna with them, and if she goes, I go. So you see how it is that, for me, to come and say I cannot help the child that I know and raised, because there is another child that came from my body that I have never seen, there is no choice to be made. Anna is my child; I do not know Miguel."

He acknowledges her story. He isn't surprised at the tale, only at the lack of emotion in the telling. It seems she is quite used to swallowing any feelings concerning her situation. Her response is most reassuring, but he still has little to no information about the young man who will be in his office the next day. "Is there anyone you know whom you could call that might tell us more about him?"

Sylvie thinks, shakes her head no. She lifts her eyes to his, "What about Anna? He might have told her something."

"Do you think Maria's family might know his parents?"

"They might have, but they are all gone. There is one aunt alive, but she is older, and I'm not sure how to contact her."

He nods, "Sylvie, can I ask a tremendous favor?" The wariness is back in the eyes. "If I send Dave to escort you, would you be there when I talk to him tomorrow?"

Panic erodes her face, but she pulls herself together and promises to come.

"One more thing, if you think of anything, anyone that might help us, will you give me a call? Here, let me program my number into your phone." Without waiting for a reply, he grasps her phone, puts his number in, and hands it back to her. She is terribly still. "Could I call someone to spend the night here with you? Maggie perhaps?" She makes no response, but he sees the tremendous effort it is taking for her to remain calm, and he dials Maggie's number. They arrange for her to come by cab to stay until morning then Rodger himself will pick her up before joining Anna for breakfast. Another hour of his day tomorrow is gone. When Maggie gets there, he makes small talk for minutes then heads out to his apartment to gather himself and prepare for the coming day. On the way he calls Detective Welden to tell him what Sylvia said about Michael's parents, and to see if there is any new information concerning on the Michael front. He is promised a report tomorrow before noon.

When he arrives at his place, he finds a visitor out front. He should have known, "Come on, you might as well come in, but you need to know that you can hang in there with your Muslim practices, but I need a stiff drink,"

Amur laughs, "Make mine bourbon and coke," then follows him into the apartment, where the two go over what little he learned from Sylvie. It is well past eleven when he shuts the door behind his uninvited guest and calls it a day. Tomorrow is coming and there is

The Wave Effect 179

much to handle. He laughs, remembering the good old days when all he had to do was to run a multifaceted international company.

Chapter 35

With the shrill announcement of the alarm, Tuesday begins. He rises, hauls himself out of bed, and in short order is headed to Claire Dailey's apartment to pick up Maggie. She is as chipper as he is silent. He is not the best of morning persons with rest. The drive to the penthouse is quick and quiet. Maggie makes a few attempts at initiating conversation, but after receiving a series of grunts for answers, she settles down to watch the road.

In the penthouse, breakfast is ready. Anna and Naydar are cutting up as young girls do, and Maggie and Ellen Hale are laughing at them as women do. He is pretending to read the morning news as he listens to the female interaction. It is relaxing in a peculiar fashion. He is dreading the upcoming session with the psychiatrist, but it appears Anna is not. He spoons his food, as giggles flood over his head, all the while searching the two faces for similarities. Something about the shape of the face seems to stand out, but he is trying too hard. He almost wishes the psychiatric session was his. He could use a little couch time with someone else analyzing and suggesting solutions to problems.

It is time to move, Phil shows up to escort them. The group includes Anna, Maggie, Rodger, and Phil. Naydar is staying behind. Rodger lets Ellen Hale know that there is a possibility that the girl's Uncle Saluar might show up, and it is okay for the two to talk.

Dr. Walker's office is a good drive from the penthouse. Maggie keeps Anna talking and relaxed, which isn't easy considering the charged silence in the forward seats. Rodger can't decide if he is apprehensive as to Anna's reaction to what she is about to learn, or scared of the fall out should she respond in a negative manner as this part of the adventure unfolds. Phil is scared. He has never felt like this about a woman, and she is a doctor, way above him on the social scale. Maggie watches amused, as she keeps check on the men and her charge with the ease of much practice.

When they arrive at Dr. Walker's offices, the reception room is empty. As per the request, the doctor has freed up her whole day to help with the upcoming problems. The secretary lets her know the patient has arrived as normal. The doctor opens the door to her office. She smiles. Everything seems like a normal day at the office. Things head toward abnormal when Rodger asks if he and Maggie can have a few moments first. The doctor pauses, her secretary freezes in the act of shutting down her computer, and a startled Phil gazes at the floor.

"Ah, sure," she says, "Penny, can you give us ten minutes?"

"Certainly, Dr. Walker." Penny sits back down behind her desk. She glances at Anna and Phil, clears her throat, and says, "Could I get you anything, coffee, tea?"

Anna shakes her head as she walks toward the magazines stacked on the end table of the office.

Phil mumbles, "Tea would be nice, thank you."

"Are you sure you don't want anything?" Penny repeats for Anna and receives a negative reply. She moves to a little anteroom to mix Phil's tea. The three sit in silence, Phil drinking his tea, Anna turning pages in a magazine about housekeeping tips, and Penny watching the two with a polite expression that seems both painted and pained.

Inside the office, Dr. Walker is brought up to date on the latest twists and turns in the Annalisel Benson case. Maggie talks about the young man, how she first knew him and the story he told. Rodger fills her in on the explosion at his office, and what will be happening this afternoon. Then he tells both of the women about the development from yesterday afternoon. Maggie is stunned. Her silence is a huge signal of astonishment. Dr. Walker is more accustomed to hiding her reactions, but she is also quiet. Into this hush comes the question, the query, "What do we tell Anna, what do we tell Naydar, and when do we disclose this?"

Dr. Walker paces the office as she thinks. She stops, looks at Maggie who shrugs. "Do you think she is ready to handle this? How would your rate her memory at this time?" These are the issues that she needs Maggie to chime in on.

Maggie taps her finger against her forehead. "I honestly think she has regained the memory loss. What this information will do to her considering the strain of her parent's death and the upcoming probate hearing, I don't know. She believes that to be pretty cut and dried, if she sees a challenge or a possible threat…, I don't have any expertise to provide an opinion."

"Your expertise is that you know the girls, both of them better or at least as well as anyone," The doctor states.

"She doesn't know Anna better than her old nanny, and she doesn't know Naydar better than her uncle," states Rodger.

"Naydar has an uncle?" Maggie's head jerks around to stare at him.

"Yes, do you remember Amur? Well he is her uncle."

"Whew, I am glad to know that, I had him pegged as a sleazy, pervert. He was always hanging around her and trying to talk with her."

"Yeah, I thought it was because he felt responsible for her, but I didn't know why, until last night. He is the reason we know that the two girls are sisters."

Doctor Walker has her information now and is ready to begin the session. "Let me work with Anna about her memory, and what she remembers and how she has processed her parent's death, then we can make a decision about what of this to share with her, and when. I'd like the two of you to wait here if that is possible, I might need you to help explain all this."

"We are all yours, Doctor," says Maggie as she pushes him toward the door. "This is Anna's day, right?"

"Uh, sure, and Phil is here in case you need to know anything from their time at the estate."

Gloria Walker's face beams for a second, then Dr. Walker settles her shoulders, walks into the reception room and greets Anna. "Come on in dear," she says. "Penny, would you acquaint our folks with the amenities of the building and answer any questions they might have, then you may leave."

Penny is only too glad to do as she is asked. She provides them with information on food and beverage locations, and hands the remote control to Phil before shutting down her computer, putting the phone on automatic answering, grabbing her purse, and leaving.

The three remaining occupants settle in for the long wait. Phil is listening to some game on his headphones, Rodger has his ever present briefcase out working on some business deals on his laptop, and Maggie alternates between pacing the floor watching the office door and stepping out in the hall to carry on conversations with colleagues over her phone.

Chapter 36

Inside the treatment room, Dr. Walker pries into Anna's memories of her childhood. They discuss her relationship with her mother, her father, and Sylvie. She sheds tears as she talks, but these are calm cleansing tears, not sobs. She is able to answer the questions put to her about the people in her inner circle, friends, even a few glimpses of the domineering grandmother. She talks about the boarding school in New York and her school in Switzerland. She tells stories of places she has been with her parents and with school chums.

Dr. Walker takes a leap and asks about her social life out of school. Anna grins, well, yes, there has been a fellow or two that she had some interest in, but nothing much came of it. There would be a few dates and some kissing and petting, but not much beyond that.

"No one that you have had sex with?" the probe continues.

"Well, you can't tell mother so, yes, there was a guy in a small tourist town in Austria that my friends and I visited, we dated and had basic, meaningless sex, more as an experiment than anything else. Silly me, I was afraid he would want to do it again so I made up an excuse to leave. I've never seen anyone so relieved." Anna chuckles.

"Let's discuss your visit to Benkulu. Tell me about the people you met there. I know you were there with your mother and father, but who else do you remember?"

"Well, when we got to the hotel, the lady that checked us in asked father if he wanted a maid assigned to the room. He did so we were introduced to Naydar. I liked her right away. She is so sweet, and always put what we wanted ahead of herself."

Doctor Walker's intense observation of the girl's body language tells her there is something more here. She probes deeper, "How did she get along with your parents?"

"I. .. it was odd, they would ask her questions about her folks and where she lived and where she grew up. It was as if they were trying to get to know everything about her. For a bit, I was jealous, then I saw what an unsophisticated sweetheart she is, she is Naydar. You have met her. What you see is what you get." A tiny smile played on her mouth as she describes the girl who is her sister.

"Back for a moment, is there anyone else you met at the hotel or the beach there in Benkulu?"

Anna pauses furls up her forehead, and asks, "Is this about the man I met on the beach? Michael Gilbeck? I met him when I was walking out of the hotel the day after we arrived at the resort. He was cute, nice, and obviously on the prowl."

"What makes you say that?"

"I might not have a lot of sexual experience, but I have enough to know when a guy has the signal out. He was fun. I thought it was intriguing that he had the same last name as Sylvie. We walked and talked for a while. I agreed to meet him again the day the storm came." Here she shrugs her shoulders, and continues, "He was there on the beach in front of the hotel after I had lunch with mother and dad. We walked for a while. It seemed strange that the water was so far out away from the shore, so we followed it. There was no one out as far as we were, and he asked if I wanted to skinny dip. Sounded like fun at the time. We both stripped down and were splashing about in the shallows when the wave appeared. We took off running naked as newborns. We didn't outrun it. I remember being pulled under, and coming up, being slammed back under again and again, until I grabbed onto a tree, that's about all I know until I regained consciousness in Maggie's little hospital. Last I saw of Michael he was trying to climb into a boat."

"Anna how do you feel about your parents?"

"I miss them, but it isn't like I was used to seeing them everyday. It is hard when I think that I will never see them again."

"Do you have any other family?"

"I have Sylvie, and now as odd as it seems, I have Naydar who is like a sister, and Maggie, and Mr. Rodger, and then our keeper Phil," she chuckles. "He is something, he would love to get away from us, but I think he is stuck till everything gets settled."

The doctor, pauses, looks at Anna and decides, "Anna, what if I told you that you do have a sister, at least a half sister?"

Anna is still. "Half sister? That would mean one of my parents had a child without the other, correct?"

"Yes"

A violent head shake precedes her comment. "They loved each other, real love, not that silly young girl stuff. I don't think they were apart long enough for anything like that to happen." She is frowning and is uncomfortable. "You wouldn't have brought this up if you didn't know something. Tell me."

"Your father went on trips for business, yes? Sometimes alone. On one of these trips, he fathered a child but didn't know of her existence until last year. Anna, you are right, they loved each other, this was a mistake, yes, but a one-time one. Would you like to talk with Mr. Rodger about how he found out about the sister?'

"Yes, does Maggie know?" The tone is indicative of a reluctance to believe what she is hearing, or a feeling of betrayal.

"Mr. Rodger found out about this last night. Maggie found out when I did about an hour ago; they have not conspired to keep this from you. Shall I let them come in and tell you how they found out about this and what they know? Please understand, you are in charge, if you are uncomfortable, and want them to leave, they will. Understood?"

She nods and the doctor opens the door, motioning the two into the office. Maggie heads straight to Anna, she hugs her tight as tears well up in the wise blue eyes. "I didn't know until a bit ago," she says.

Anna's expression is one of braced courage. "Tell me what you know and how you found out." Her request is aimed at Rodger. He sits on the sofa, beside her, Maggie on the other side.

"I am going out to let you talk. If you need me or when you are ready to continue with your session, tap on the door." The last is directed straight to Anna to let her know she is the one in charge.

Phil looks up to see her and scrambles to his feet. "Is she okay? Why are you here when she is in with them?"

"You don't know?"

"Know what?"

Doctor Walker resets to merely Gloria Walker, no title. Gloria Walker wants to share, but Doctor Walker can't. So instead of talking about what is going on in the next room, they make meaningless chatter about the Yankees, the NFL, learning to fly a jet, and whatever else pops into their heads, all the while watching the door as if it is about to explode.

Then it does. "What?" comes out to them through the sound proof walls. Dr. Walker stands and heads for the door which flies open almost hitting her in the face. Anna charges out followed by Maggie and Rodger. Her beaming face tells the doctor she is taking the news well. Phil is the one who looks bewildered and out of the loop. "Phil, she *is* my sister. I have a sister and it is my heart sister. What wonderful news. I have a family. I am not alone."

"Who, what?" Phil is lost and swimming hard to stay with the current.

"Naydar, she is my sister. Isn't it wonderful how life can take away and then, in such a strange way, give back?" She grabs his hands and dances him around the room. The relief, felt by all except Phil who has no idea what he should feel, is palpable. Anna herself brings Phil in to the informed circle. She is anxious to share the news.

Doctor Walker brings her down a peg, "Calm down a bit," she commands. "Did you finish informing her?"

Maggie and Rodger look at each other and that says it all. "Okay, lets all go back in and finish where we are, so we can see where we need to go next." Everyone except Phil heads for the door. Anna looks back and grabs his hand pulling him in with her.

Inside, the group sits and waits as Rodger goes into the Michael story and the upcoming meeting in his office. "We have a few things to decide," he starts when he is interrupted by the doctor.

"No, she has a few things to decide. Let's define what the issues are and what type of time frame we have."

Rodger starts over, "Naydar, do we tell her, and when, before or after the hearing on Thursday? Then do you feel up to watching my meeting with Michael this afternoon? He would not need to know you were there."

"As a fact checker?" Anna's mood is almost playful.

"I am at your disposal for this day and Thursday I will be at the hearing," Doctor Walker assures her.

"I am for telling Naydar now, right now."

"That might not be best for her. Let us work on that a bit. When is the meeting with Michael?"

"It is at 3:30 in my office. Amur, Naydar's Uncle, will be there as well as Sylvie and Maggie,"

"Amur is Naydar's Uncle?" Anna's head shakes back and forth, "There is so much I don't know."

"And you deserve answers, so let's go over everything we have uncovered for you today, discuss how you feel about it all, and then make the decisions. Maybe we can develop a list of questions you want to have answered?" The doctor is back in charge.

Rodger agrees, "I think we will head back to the office and prepare for the visit. You can let us know when you are ready, then Phil will bring you if you decide to be there."

" As for Naydar," Maggie chimes in, "It might be wise to make up a plan for springing this on her. She will have a lot to assimilate. The father she knew wasn't her father. The father she had just come to know is dead, and she has a sister. That's a lot to take in. We might need a plan or you might need a plan. I have to go rejoin my team tomorrow."

"What!" comes out of at least three mouths at once. Maggie smiles at them, hugs Anna and then states, "I'm needed elsewhere. You are fine, but if you need me, call. I'll be here tonight and will see you tomorrow morning, then I am off."

Anna's face falls, "You are part of my family."

"Yep, and always will be, no worries."

Maggie and the silent Rodger step out, take the elevator down to the street and hail a cab.

The Wave Effect 189

Chapter 37

As they step into the cab, he instructs the cabby to drop them at an exclusive downtown restaurant. She gives a "what are you doing" look at him. "Lunch" is the reply. A sly turn of the head tells him she ain't buying what he is selling. The distance is short and it is less than a half hour before they are seated in the swank confines of one of New York's finest, with cocktails on the table and a lovely salad with lobster and shrimp on the way.

"Okay, what is this all about?" she asks.

"My way of saying thank you for everything you have done and everything you have shown us how to do. Salud!" he touches his glass to hers in toast. "When did you find out you had to leave?"

"Evelyn called Sunday and told me about the new assignment, but I felt I might be needed here for this first couple of days. She and Bobby are setting up in Somalia, a new place there. Its a bear to set up, and they are having fits with the government officials who are suspicious of anyone coming in. Well, you can guess."

"This going to be a safe place for you? I don't know much about that region. Carl was our expert on all things foreign, but seems I remember something about them not caring for women being in charge of anything."

"You are overstating, but we will wear head coverings. They have an epidemic devastating the area. At this point, they would welcome the Rockettes if they were free and could help."

The chuckles break the somber atmosphere and they move to more immediate problems. "How do you think this afternoon will go for Sylvie?" He asks.

She is a bit surprised that he is concerned. "I don't know, she is all in Anna's corner, but this is her baby and though she has not laid eyes on him in all these years, he is part of her. It is going to be hard."

"Is that what kept you here?"

She smiles, "In part, she is so alone, has been. Maria was her only tie, and of course Anna, but now it is her. Maria is gone and Anna is grown; she doesn't require a nanny. I think someone needs to be here to hang onto Sylvie, yes, but I also admit I am super curious about when Naydar will be informed, and how she will take the news. Do you think Amur has already told her?"

"No, I think he will want to see what Anna does before he takes that step. Do you think it should be him who does the telling?"

"Oh, he should be there for sure. That is the first thing that child will need, a source she trusts to backup all she is learning. Poor kid, I feel for her. Its not going to be an easy path for any of them."

"I was shocked to hear Anna so enthusiastic, I was a bit hesitant to tell her."

"This is why Doctor Walker wants us out of the way so she can calm Anna down and see if the reaction is real, or part of missing grief."

"Seemed real to me, but then I am not a trained medical person."

"Stages of grief make it hard to evaluate this sort of news this close to a tragic event. I have my fingers crossed and my toes are twitching."

Rodger relaxes, first time in three days, and his best medicine is running out. They complete the meal, he looks at his watch, and grimaces. "Time?" she asks.

"I'm afraid so," is the reply. A cab is waiting for them when they depart, the next stop Benson Enterprises. It is 2:10, and Amur is sitting in the reception area making small talk with Claire Dailey. James is sitting on her desk listening while he pretends to be engrossed in legal papers he has in his hands.

"Anyone else here?" Asks Rodger.

"Sylvie is in my office," James answers. "Amur has fixed the video feed so that we can all gather there and watch. Are Anna and Doctor Walker on the way?"

"I don't know. Amur, is there a way you can make that feed available on a phone or tablet?"

"Sure, why?"

"I am wondering if it might be better if Sylvie were close like in the closet or bathroom and then be ready if I needed to summon her."

"Better idea," interrupts Claire, "Have Sylvie here. We will watch together. Then if you want her involved give me a signal and I'll send her in."

"Yes, I like that. What sort of signal?"

Amur smiles at the two. "Make it super simple. Walk to the computer and punch up NOW."

Rodger and Claire look at him as if he cured cancer. Claire starts to James' office to explain it to Sylvie, when Maggie steps up. "I'll go sit with her and tell her what the current plan is."

Claire's area seems too small for some reason, so Rodger and Amur move to his office. James stays with Claire. "We have everyone spread out," he comments. "I hope you don't get confused as to where everyone is." He leans closer, "Where do you want to go on our honeymoon?" he steals a quick kiss.

"Away from New York City," is the quick answer.

Inside of Rodger's office, the conversation focuses on how Anna took the news and what Amur said to Naydar. "Do you think she is ready to hear that Anna is her sister?"

"I don't know. I wish her mother were here."

" I wish both mothers were here, then I could go back to being my grumpy old self and work on mergers instead of teenage angst."

Amur laughs, "Women, how do they do it? How do they keep their composure when every card in the deck is falling on the floor?"

"Don't know." Rodger admits. "I bet I have said those words more in the last month than all the rest of my life. Where are you going to watch this little episode? James' office with the group or Carl's office?"

"That, my friend depends upon how I am greeted by Miss Benson. I don't want her upset as she watches, but I would like to be close enough to prompt her if some controversy comes up."

"Doctor Walker is coming with her, maybe she can help you decide."

"Phil coming too?"

"Yes, why?"

"I think the good doctor might be distracted."

Rodger's eyes squeeze into a frown, then relax, "Oh, I hadn't noticed. Want me to send him somewhere else?"

"No. I would, however, like them to get here soon so we can check the radar, so to speak."

The worlds are fresh from his mouth when the elevator door sounds. Amur steps up quickly to the computer, punches a key and a video of the reception area lights up. The elevator opens and out steps the three they expected. They go to meet them and everyone heads to James' office except James and Claire. There, it is confrontation time between Anna and her sister's uncle. The rest feel out of place except Dr. Walker and Maggie who are quick to observe Anna's flushed face. Amur holds out his hand, she looks at it, looks at him, smiles and gives him a big hug. Everyone is a little bit startled, but not as much as Amur. He is not a hugger. Sylvie steps up and shakes his hand which breaks the spell.

"Okay everyone, it is 2:40. I suggest we all get into our places. Maggie, you are going to stay here with Dr. Walker and Anna, correct? And Sylvie, you will stay here until Michael arrives, then you will join Claire. James will be with me. That leaves you two guys. Where do you want to be?"

Phil shrugs and Maggie pushes him into a chair.

"Miss Anna, can I watch with you?" Amur's soft words belie his churning emotions.

Anna takes his hands, leads him to the couch and sits him down beside her. "I understand it was you who gave me my best gift ever. Please sit down and tell me about my sister."

Rodger looks to Maggie and the smile that breaks upon her face. He leaves, heads to his office, motioning for James to follow. Everyone is in place and now the waiting game begins. The legal office is full of soft conversation, but the COO's office is silent. James strains to listen for the elevator, while Rodger sits in front of his computer and watches the reception area.

Chapter 38

Every sound is louder than usual, every creak raises attention. The two men wait and wonder if Amur is correct. He said Michael will be anxious, nervous, early. The ten minutes between the separation into groups and the telephone ring seems hours long. Rodger answers the call, "No, it is fine, send him on up." James nods and calls Claire to give her a warning, while Rodger calls Maggie. Then all goes silent as everyone waits. The bell sounds, the door opens, and Claire buzzes the office. "Your 3:30 appointment is here,"

"Have him wait, I'll be right with him," is the answer. He glances at his watch. James holds up six fingers. They talk about a business deal that they finished years ago as if it were of major importance to keep sound in the room. Minutes tick by like thick molasses dripping into a cup. At the six minute mark, James nods and opens the door.

"Mr. Gilbeck, sorry to keep you waiting, but you are a bit early. Come on in, did you bring any representation with you? This Is Mr. Stanton, the head of our legal department." James ushers the angry young man into the office where Rodger sits behind the desk, all of his attention focused on the computer.

Michael Gilbeck is tall, almost as tall as Rodger. His frame is sturdier than Sylvie's, and his jaw is squared, but the blue eyes and brown hair are reminiscent of his mother. He is glaring at the two men as if it is them who should be uncomfortable.

Rodger stands, holds out one hand and with the other indicates that Michael should sit. James takes his place to the side of the indicated chair. Michael looks daggers at the offered hand, and pauses as if trying to decide if he will continue standing or take the offered chair. Rodger shrugs and sits, folds his hands and watches Michael. Silence fills the room, then Michael squares his shoulders, and sits. "I want to know where my wife is being held, and why I have not been notified of her condition," he begins.

Rodger's head turns a tad. He glances at James who shakes his head and then turns back to the young man before him. "I have no idea what you are talking about." His voice is calm and cool. There is nothing to grant any opening. "Who is your wife, and why would you think we know where she might be?"

"You know very well who my wife is. Anna Benson is my wife, and I know that my former lawyer told you that."

"He said something along those lines, but we had no reason to believe he knew that to be true."

Now a frown appears on Michael's face, "What do you mean?"

"We were provided with no evidence of any marriage, no evidence of any kind of engagement," chimes in James. "Why don't you provide us with your documentation."

"The storm erased any documents and you would know that. My wife's memory is also impaired. I don't know if she would remember even our courtship."

"Annalisel's memory is fine. However, she does not remember any wedding or talk of such. So without her or someone else backing your claim, well, I think you must understand our position." Rodger tapes his fingers and waits.

"Her mother arranged the marriage. We were wed the night before the storm," Michael spouts.

James looks at him and says, "Really, because now we do have a witness, the maid who worked at the hotel. She would be able to corroborate your version. But she has not indicated anything of the sort. When did you meet Anna?"

"We met in Germany,"

"Has Anna ever been to Germany?" James turns to Rodger.

"Not that I am aware of."

"Maybe it was Austria? I'm not sure, we have been writing for years."

"Good, good, then you will have some letters to produce, right?"

"No, I left them when I left home."

Two sets of eyebrows raise on this one. "You did? Okay, and where is home?"

"I live in Germany. I have been at a private school in Munich."

"And your parents? Who are they?"

James presses in his dry lawyer's voice.

"Mr. and Mrs. Ruggart Gilbeck, why is that important? I am over twenty one, an adult."

In the office, the reveal brings no response, but in the reception area where Claire and Sylvie sit staring at the monitor, there is a strong reaction. Sylvie gasps, covers her face with her hands. Tears trickle down her cheeks as she stares at her son. No doubt remains; this is her child.

Back in the office, the men look at the intruder, "Okay, Mr. Gilbeck, shall we bring Anna here to confront your story?"

Michael stares, starts to speak, and then says, "Her mother invited me to join them."

"Why would she do that?" the soft tone belies the intensity of the question.

"She is my mother." This reply even has Rodger blinking.

"Let me see if I can put things in order," says James. "Your mother Maria Benson, invited you to meet her daughter, your sister, and approved of your marriage to her? Is that what you are contending here?"

"No, Yes," Michael's head twists as he tries to both confront and avoid both men.

"Both of us were quite familiar with Maria Benson. She would never have allowed her daughter to marry her half brother. So what is the story? How did you meet up with the Bensons?"

"I studied Benson enterprises for years. No matter what you say, I know we are kin. I heard they were going to be at that resort. I wanted to get to know them, but he wouldn't agree to see me. I waited on Anna, I thought I could get in through her. Look, they are part of my family, and they are wealthy. I went to see if I could get to know them, maybe become part of the company. It is only fair. They owe me." Now the voice is octaves higher and strident. He is pushing his words out like missiles intended to blow apart the unfair world.

The door opens, and Sylvie confronts the man child she birthed so many years age. "Maria Benson was not your mother, I am." Her words are flat; the tremor in the voice is the emotional indicator. Sylvie is holding on by a thread.

The room is devoid of any sound until the buzzer at the desk sounds startling all. Rodger pick up the call so that he and only he can hear. It is Claire to the rescue. She says nothing but listens as he pretends conversation, "Yes, I remember. Can't that wait? I see, no no, we will be right out." He replaces the phone. "Sorry, but there is an urgent matter that Mr. Stanton and I must deal with. If you will wait, we will return, meanwhile, feel free to stay here."

They walk to the door and let themselves out. The remaining two stand staring at each other. If they are aware the others left, no one could prove it. At the reception area, James stops, kisses Claire on top of her head as thanks. Rodger smiles, waves and lets himself into the other room where everyone's attention is on the monitor. He walks to Anna and stands beside the couch between her and Maggie. Phil is seated beside Dr. Walker who looks as if she has been hit square in the gut by a haymaker. Amur sits on Anna's other side, watching each player endure the silence.

Chapter 39

In the office, Michael stares at Sylvie, mouth open, eyes filled with hurt and confusion. Sylvie stares back not knowing what to say or how to begin. Therefore it is Michael who breaks the void. "You, you are my mother?" His head shakes slowly side to side, "Why? Who are you?" he pauses, again silence reigns. Then softer, "Why?"

Sylvie's lips tremble, her fight to regain composure is obvious. "I had no choice."

"Why?" the question is stronger and less vulnerable.

Sylvie sighs, she moves to the couch to the seat James had vacated, facing Michael. "Do you want the end, the beginning, or all of the story?"

"I want the whole story. Who are you and why do you say you are my mother? I thought Anna's mother Maria was my mother."

"No, Maria Benson is, was my cousin and my best friend. We grew up spending much time with our grandparents. Her mother and my mother were sisters. Maria's maiden name was Wurzer, mine was Gilbeck. My father was a strict constructionist. He believed that the man was head of the house and the women were there to serve."

"Well, yes, that is the way the Bible sets the household," he agrees.

Sylvie's frown leads him to wonder what she believes. "Yes, so you know about the way I was raised. The only time I felt free was when I was at Maria's or at grandmother's house. I tried hard to please my father to little or no avail. I studied hard in school making good marks, had few friends, and, of course, there were no boys allowed. I graduated to the University at age seventeen."

She pauses and Michael stares. In the other room, a tense Anna is listening and learning along with Michael. There are at least three in the room who wonder how all this is affecting Michael and two concerned with how it is affecting Anna. One among the listeners is crying inside for Sylvie, the strong, hard shelled Sylvie.

"What happened when you went to the university," sneers Michael, "Get yourself pregnant?" His voice is harsh, his words drip with sarcasm. Sylvie draws back and up.

"Have you no schooling at all?" she answers, "A woman can't get herself pregnant. She has to thank a man for that."

"Ouch," mutters Maggie. Phil swallows a chuckle which gains him a poke in the ribs from the good doctor.

"Yes, I was easy prey. I had no knowledge of men or relationships and I was pregnant three months into my stay."

"Why not abort me? Why have me if you didn't want me?" His words are like the wail of one too familiar with pain.

"You were raised by the cousins of my father. Do you think anyone consulted me? Do you not know I had no choice? Do you have any female kin? Would they be allowed to say abort or keep? Would they?"

Michael looks to the floor as if there might be an answer written there, but there is none and when he looks up there is a noticeable change in his eyes; the gleam is for her pain, not his. "Would you ?" The tone is soft, the words smoother.

"I don't know, I remember when they put you in my arms, I never wanted to give you back. I got to keep you for one whole day, then my father took you away. And today I see you again. My Miguel, that is the name that I gave you. You were so tiny, so cute, and so fussy." Her memories trickle down her face as the words drip from her mouth. She isn't sure when her wall went up, but the crash is imminent. She continues to stare, her head rocking back and forth, her arms wrapped around her chest as if to stave off any rejection.

In the other office, Anna is minutes away from rescuing Sylvie from this pain. Doctor Walker sees it and takes the girl out to the hallway to talk to her away from the scene. Rodger and Phil are watching as if drawn into a play that they cannot believe, but they cannot walk away from. Maggie the tenderhearted is ready to yank a knot in Michael and rip his mother from his presence. James and Claire watch, James thinking legal, Claire thinking of her son and what it would have been like to never know day to day where he was or who he was. Would she have looked at every male and wondered is he the child I lost?

Michael is stunned, he has no idea how to respond. He reaches forward, then pulls his arms back into his body, "Did you want me?"

"Not until you were born, then yes, I wanted you. I begged everyday for a solid week for them to bring you back to me. You were the best excuse my father had to get rid of me. It worked, I never saw him again. There I was, no place to live, no job, no one to help with bills or food. I had no chance, sometimes I wonder what would have happened to you if I had tried to keep you? I talked myself into believing that whereever you were, you were better off. They told me you were with a cousin of Father's. That they wanted a child and would give you a home and all the advantages that I couldn't. I believed them, I had to, but I have never had one day that I didn't think of you and wonder."

"Maybe, but not enough to try and find me?"

"For what purpose? To disrupt your life? To cause an upheaval and make problems you never asked for?"

"Maybe, or maybe you just didn't care if I needed you. I have wondered so many times who my mother was, why she gave me to these people who didn't want a child. They wanted a puppet, someone with strings they could jerk around and control. They are so angry that they aren't wealthy. It is their right as good, righteous people to be successful and rich, and since they aren't, I have to be. I was told that my mother was connected to Benson Enterprises and that the Bensons were wealthy even though they were nowhere near as pious as Gilbecks. It is their American connections that give them advantages, although everyone knows that Germans are smarter, even Swedes like my mother are smarter than those ridiculous Americans. It isn't fair!" His voice is back to strident, his face is flushed.

"Your premise has a hint of truth. The Benson's were American and rich, but they disowned Carl because he wouldn't be what they wanted him to be, sort of like what you are saying. He went out alone, without help and made his company into the international success it is on his own. Of course, none of that is possible without his education and background. Carl Benson was a smart man, and he loved a

The Wave Effect 201

beautiful smart woman. She gave me hope, support and love although his family never liked our relationship. Anna has been the baby I raised in your place. I wish things were better for you, tell me what you do, what you studied, what you dream of doing?"

"I grew up much like you, studied, made good grades, went to private schools and University. My adopted parents knew they would never achieve the station in life they sought, so they turned to me to be the instrument of success. Father told me I had a connection with Benson Enterprises, and I was pushed into studies that focused on trade, legal language of deal making, and all sorts and forms of energy. I've been preparing to take a prominent place in this company for *years*, and Benson wouldn't even receive me. He had the front desk at the resort tell me he was on vacation, and I should call his office in New York and make an appointment." He inhales and the blood vessels in his neck enlarge.

Rodger looks at Maggie, "Should I go in and break this meeting up?"

She shakes her head, "No, she's got this."

He looks at her sideways, Phil's eyes enlarge, and, in silence, he disagrees.

"And now, because you failed at your first attempt to make a contact, you give up? Didn't you inherit any of my stubbornness? Miguel?"

"*Michael!*"

"Michael, are you so limited that you can't get a good job somewhere besides Benson Enterprises? If you are as educated as you say, I'd think you would be a catch for many places. Why only here?"

"I… I am owed."

"Really? Why? I guess I could see that if you thought yourself the son of one of the owners, but now you know you aren't, then why?"

There is a significant pause in the conversation. Michael is digesting her words, his situation. He looks her up and down.

"Think, Michael, you just told me all the areas of study you have been through to prepare, weren't you instructed in the making of presentations? Wasn't that one of the skills you enumerated?"

"Yes."

"Well, if I asked would you prepare a presentation on why an international energy company would be lucky to have you as an employee?"

"I could, but what would you do with it?"

"If it is any good, I'd show it to the new owners of the company and their officers. But only if it is good."

James opens the door to his office looks at Rodger and nods. They both agree they need to find Anna and see what the doctor thinks about the situation that is growing stickier by the minute.

Doctor Walker and Anna are still discussing the practicality of interfering in the reunion when the two men approach. "Dr. Walker, do you think it would be advantageous to break in on the meeting," James points to Rodger's office.

"Anna wants to be a part and I think you need to let her. But it must be as the owner of the company. Give Michael notice that she isn't a potential date, she is the one with the final say."

The men turn and look at each other, this is the first time they have ever considered this.

"Will you be accompanying us?"

"No, as Maggie likes to say, she's got this."

It is obvious that the two aren't convinced, but Anna's head inches up and she nods at the men, "Let's go."

Chapter 40

As they open the door, two heads twist to the sound. Sylvie's face goes through a plethora of emotions: surprise, confusion, fear, relief. Michael appears as if he is caught with his hand in the cookie jar. Both of them stand stiff and silent. Rodger walks to his desk and turns to introduce Michael to Anna. Anna holds up her hand. "We need no introduction. Hello Michael, I am so glad you made it out of the storm okay. I'd shake your hand, but I am still recuperating from several broken bones and well, I don't shake hands right now. Last I saw of you you were climbing into a boat."

Michael smiles at her memory, "Yes, I was hit in the back by that thing first, everything was groggy after that. How did you make it through the storm?"

"To tell the truth, I don't know. I must have grabbed hold of something, but I remember seeing you lifting into the boat and the next thing I remember is waking up in the clinic, nothing between. I wish I did, I'd love to thank whoever pulled me out of the water. I bet you would too, or did you?"

"No, I remember the time in the boat, but not the actual rescue. I got to the clinic and began to ask about you. They told me someone fitting your description was there, but she had no memory therefore they had no idea who she was. I tried to make them take me to you, but they wouldn't."

"I did lose my memory for a bit, but it has come back now except for the time in the water. Thank you for trying to find me. That was sweet of you."

The is a pause in the conversation, Michael is searching for words. "Do you remember before the wave?"

"Heavens yes, I don't know why we didn't suspect something when the beach was so long. I mean it wasn't as if I hadn't been on that beach for days, and on it with you just a few days before. We should have guessed. But then, if anyone should have known it would have been the people who lived there, and they didn't seem to suspect anything." Anna laughs at her remark and Michael sort of joins in. The remaining three simply stand as the words go back and forth. "Come on everyone, let's sit down and talk, looking up at all of you is hurting my neck." Again Anna chuckles at her wee joke, this time everyone except Sylvie joins in.

"Anna, you should know, this is Miguel,"

"Michael."

"Michael, my son. He is your cousin once removed. I wasn't sure until today, but I am sure now."

Anna's face is calm, composed as opposed to her nanny's. Sylvie is exhausted, her body droops as Rodger leads her to a place on the couch next to the girl who is becoming a woman before their eyes. James motions for Michael to take a chair opposite the women and he sits next to him. Rodger sits in the front of the group.

Michael makes a gesture of "who knew" with his hands and remains quiet. Anna surveys the room, clears her voice and asks Michael, "Did you know about her, I mean that she was your mother?"

"No, I found out only minutes ago." He looks around, his foot tapping the floor, then he squares his shoulders and admits, "I thought my mother was your mother."

Anna looks hard at him, "You thought we were siblings? You sure have an interesting way of introducing yourself to your sister."

Michael stares at the carpet, his foot retaining the tap. "Yeah, It was stupid of me, I am sorry."

Sylvie's face lights up at the confession. She reaches to touch his hand and he lets her. Mother and son smile at each other for the first time. For the first time, there is a real connection.

Anna nods her approval, pats Sylvie, and says, "We aren't brother and sister, but we are kin and you will be welcome in my house always."

The two men are watching wthout comment. James clears his throat., "I assume this means there will not be a challenge to the estate settlement on Thursday from you?"

"No, no challenge, but I would like to be there."

Sylvie looks at Rodger, but it is Anna who answers his request. "You must join us with your mother."

It appears this meeting is over. Anna suggests that Sylvie take Michael back to Claire's apartment for some time together. Within minutes they are gone. The rest of the group joins those remaining in the office. Anna says to Claire, "I hope you don't mind that I sent them to your place. Right now it seemed to be easiest solution."

Claire looks at James, "It's fine, just remember, boss, you owe me one."

Anna laughs then settles down to determine what the rest of this day will contain. She has endured a lot of emotional stress and exhaustion is approaching. "So what is next?"

Dr. Walker eyes her patient, "For you, some alone time, food and rest. Everything else will have to wait."

"But what about Naydar, she doesn't know yet. We must tell her."

"I would like to be with you when you do that Miss Anna, and I cannot tonight. Could you wait till morning? Please?" asks Amur.

"I think it would be best for her to have her uncle there," the doctor agrees. "Let's go back to the office and work on processing what you have learned today. We will have you home by seven or eight. How is that?"

Anna agrees as does Rodger. The doctor, Phil, Anna and Amur leave. Claire invites Rodger, James, and Maggie to supper, but Rodger and Maggie decline. It is six thirty. They want a little time alone before the circus starts anew.

"Do you absolutely have to leave tomorrow."

"Yes, but the plane is scheduled at three so we will have the morning if you need me for anything."

"You have no idea," mutters Rodger Madden, COO and interim CEO of Benson Enterprises. "No idea at all."

Supper is mixed, there is the joy of being together and the dread of being apart. They share the joy with all in the penthouse. Phil announces that he has the plane ready for tomorrows flight. Maggie looks at him and then at Rodger, "What flight?"

"Phil and Dave will be taking you to your new station in our plane so you can sleep and be rested when you arrive. Tonight you and I are leaving this motley crew and having one last night on the town before we have to start again." Rodger lifts his glass.

Naydar who is delighted to have company in the house after a stark day, lifts her glass also, "To Ms. Maggie, the best doctor ever."

Supper is over at nine and Rodger take Maggie away. Phil takes Dr. Walker home as the two girls talk. Anna is bursting to tell Naydar about the whole day, but she sticks with the plan and only discusses Michael. By ten Anna is yawning and Naydar insists she go to bed. Tuesday is over at last.

Maggie and Rodger visit his favorite places. They eat , they talk , they laugh, then they head down to the water, to the spot he first took her in New York, and they sit is silence. He reaches for her hand but words crumble in his mouth. And so they sit.

Chapter 41

Wednesday dawns, Maggie wakes and shakes the cobwebs out. She checks out the area and then, startled, finds herself in bed with Rodger Madden. Her face softens, she slips out of the bed, redresses, leaves a note to let him know where she will be, and calls a cab.

By the time he wakes up she has slipped into her room at the penthouse, showered, dressed, and is ready to face the day. He staggers out of bed, finds her note, snickers at the wording, and begins his day. The plan is to have brunch at the penthouse, but before the brunch, there will be the reveal to Naydar, then food and a celebration of sisters, to be followed by a farewell for Maggie. That is the plan, he prays that this plan manages to hang together.

He is at the penthouse by nine. It is Amur who opens the door. Naydar is on the couch beside Anna. Mrs. Hale is checking on the meal and working on setting up the table, and Maggie, his friend Maggie is in the dining room working along side. He swallows his laughter and greets everyone.

"Are Michael and Sylvie coming," asks Maggie?

"I think so, but I haven't heard anything this morning," is his reply. "I guess we could call?"

"No," Maggie responds, "Let's let them set their agenda today."

Rodger nods, and they join the group in the living area.

Amur pours everyone a small glass of champagne from a bottle he has purchased this morning. "A toast – To my two beautiful nieces."

"Here, here," says Rodger, lifting his glass. Everyone joins in. Naydar sips, lowers her glass, and says, "Nieces? Two nieces?"

Amur smiles, tilts his glass toward Anna and says, "Would you like to do the honors?"

Anna beams, "Naydar, according to the DNA tests done on your hair and mine, we are sisters. Welcome to the family."

Amur leans toward Anna, "And the same to you."

Naydar is looking from one to the other, mouth slack, eyes wide, trying to determine if this is some sort of elaborate joke. She sees nothing to indicate it is, but she turns to check with Maggie and then with Rodger. "This is true? I have a sister? I am family?" The last is directed to Anna.

Anna's beaming face is the final proof she needs.

She drops the almost full glass and covers her face.

"Naydar, aren't you happy? Oh please, please be happy." Anna reaches for the shaking girl's hands, gives up and gathers her into a hug, the two rocking together on the couch as Naydar cries and Anna comforts.

Maggie heads toward the girls until she receives the "not yet" shake of the head by Rodger. "Come, come little sister, we have been through so much, lost so much, but here we are, and this is a gain, a big gain. You will always be my sister, my friend, the one who was there when I was lost. I will always be your sister, your friend, the one who is here and will be here, as long as there is an us."

Everyone feels. For some the emotion of the moment is too much, the feelings are weighty. The doorbell rings and everyone jumps. In walks Phil with flowers for the table and two bouquets for the girls. "Happy sister day," he says, and everyone laughs, breaking the spell. Naydar and Anna take their flowers and head to the bedroom to "wash faces". The remainder stand there and talk of nothing worth remembering until the doorbell rings again and Mrs. Hale ushers in Michael and Sylvie.

Sylvie looks around and asks, "Where are my girls?"

"In that bedroom," points Maggie. "They are talking it out."

"Nonsense," Sylvie pushes past the group and goes into the room. Shouts of glee indicate this is a good idea, and shortly, the door opens and the girls emerge with Sylvie, who is reminding them that they have company and this is no way to act toward visitors.

Soon they are all gathered around the table for a brunch fit for royalty. There is laughter, joy, joking, and little sense of what the rest of the day will bring. Maggie refuses to dwell upon her departure. Several others attempt to own that position, but at least two are dreading this coming evening. Phil is not partaking in the toasts, and his boss is quiet, very quiet.

Sylvie takes a pause in the conversation to ask about Maggie's new assignment. Maggie smiles and begins describing the place, "It is in a small Somalian village. All I know is that Bobby calls it steaming and that is bad coming from someone from the desert part of Australia. There is a epidemic going on there, this is one carried by insects of which they have tons. We need to nurse the ones that are sick, help the researchers discover which bugger is causing this, and teach preventive medicine to those not infected, all within a perilous governmental situation. That is what this organization is all about."

"What if you catch the stuff?" asks Naydar.

"Then Evelyn and Bobby will be taking care of me until I am removed from the area. Don't worry, the organization takes really good care of all of us who are willing to work these missions."

"I bet," mutters Phil. "I've been in Somalia. Very unstable country if you ask me."

Maggie smiles, draws herself up and answers, "Most of the countries we serve are unstable; it is part of what makes them unable or unwilling to devote resources to those who are sick or weak. Sad. Let's talk of happier things. Girls, what will be your first girls' trip? Somewhere special to each of you?" And with that the conversation heads to a happier foundation.

When everyone is stuffed, the real day begins, Rodger leaves for the office after reminding everyone they are having a farewell party at the Waldorf Astoria at six sharp. Michael and Sylvie are headed to Benson Enterprises to work with James on the probate hearing scheduled for tomorrow. Phil will round up Dave check out the plane and the flight plans, then pick up Gloria Walker for the party.

Maggie is checking her baggage and any space that might be hiding articles she will need mid flight when her phone rings.

"I want to come and get you early say about three? Or maybe, I could have Dave drive you on over if you are all caught up. There is a matter we need to discuss," Rodger explains.

"Last night?" jokes Maggie.

"What about last night?" he answers.

"Anything *you* want to discuss?"

There is a comfortable pause, then he says, "No, this is about your mission and what support we might be able to offer from here. I want to have you come and let us know who to contact, what is needed in the way of supplies, and how we go about securing whatever you ask for."

"Well, I am packed up here, if you want I can take a cab, or Dave can drop me by whatever is easiest."

"Dave will be there in a few minutes. Bring your bag, I'll take you to the party, if that is okay with you." He remembers the last order he gave her and grins.

"I'll be ready," she answers and goes to tell the girls and Mrs. Hale where she is going.

"Oh, I thought we would have you all day," states Anna.

"You need to have a long sweet dose of sister time," Maggie replies, "I am never going to be further than your phone."

Dave drops her off at the office and she and Rodger spend the next few hours going over suppliers and supplies. They order in a sandwich and split that between them, as they continue working through possible scenarios a while longer. James pops in to tell them all is going well so far on the estate, and to tell Maggie how much he and Claire will miss her. "You aren't coming to my party?" she asks in surprise.

"Oh, we will be there, even if it means I have to work late tonight. Right, Boss."

Rodger gives him the sour eye. "Yeah, whatever it takes, all of us will be at your farewell party."

James exists laughing, and Rodger suggests a slide down to the river. The two head to the spot that is now their place in New York. Some how the water draws them. The movement as the small ripples slapping the edge of the earth draws them. They stare at the water, the bustling city, the masses of people headed everywhere, anything but the other person on the bench. "I wish you didn't have to go," finally he speaks his heart.

"I wish you could go too," is the answer. "You have business here, mine is there. But I can still wish."

He nods and in silence they sit and look, each inhaling the scent of the other, the special presence of a special presence. "I guess we better go clean up for your party." He takes her hand and lifts her up. They head to the garage and his car and his apartment.

Chapter 42

Maggie's party is everything Rodger had hoped, filled with flowers, friends, cheering speeches, and rocking music. Considering the amount of time the hotel has had to pull the event together, this party is a rousing success. Everyone Maggie has met in America is in attendance including the staff from both the estate at Utley and the Penthouse. James is hanging on to Claire who is tearful even through all the gaiety. Phil escorts the good Doctor Gloria, who for once is not fixated on Anna's reactions. Although early for New York, the room is full, and the party goers make every effort to make this last night a great one.

The food, yes, food again, is fantastic, and after the meal, everyone partakes in a roast of Maggie Burrell. Rodger has the foresight to have the whole thing filmed (without her knowledge). He will send it to Africa.

First up to speak is Mrs. Hale who merely acknowledges what a wonderful guest Maggie has been even if she is sometimes a bit outspoken. The staff from Utley cheer her on. When Michael says how she managed to remain neutral in his misunderstandings, everyone claps. Phil is the first to "roast". He takes the mic from Michael, and says, "Really, do you actually know the lady? She can be many things, stubborn, opinionated, flat out bossy, but neutral? Anybody ever see this woman not take sides? If I were you, I'd be watching my backside. When I first met Maggie, she was ordering me, my co pilot and my boss around as if it were *her* plane that we were flying into a nightmare. She doesn't know, poor soul, that a pilot is always in charge of the people on his plane, at least while in flight. Then, as if that weren't enough, when we set down, she starts in like the drill sergeant at Parris Island, ordering me and Dave to unload the plane, hey you, that is what minions are for. Man, was I glad when we got clearance to take off leaving her there. Of course, it didn't hurt that we were leaving the boss too. Got back to Australia, had me some relaxing

The Wave Effect 215

plans. Next thing I know, I am working ferry service for a dang hospital this one," he points to Maggie, "has set up. And, if she hasn't changed in the last few hours, I expect she will be ordering me around in the plane tonight. At least it is night so hopefully she will sleep, but I don't count on it." Roars of laughter mingle with Phil's speech. Maggie blushes and tries to look insulted but fails.

Next up is James. He recalls his first meeting with the lady doctor. "I don't know quite what I was expecting, but I had heard many descriptive phrases from my colleague while they were in Indonesia that left me unprepared for this one. I was expecting, let's see, a momma bear, a ruthless dictator, a relentless worker, a demanding head of operations, in other words, some sort of cross between Wonder Woman and Mother Mary. I walk into the office and here sits this tiny creature, beautiful smile, graceful manner, and I am thinking, who are you? Seriously, Dr. Burrell, it is an honor for both Claire and me to know you and a privilege to name you as a friend. If ever you wish to change professions and become a lawyer, I would hire you in a heartbeat to represent me."

Maggie is delighted with the descriptions and turns to frown at Rodger, but the laughter bursting from her gives her away.

The night is progressing as hoped and one at a time, the rest of the party give Maggie props, except the sisters who double team her. Anna takes the podium with Naydar at her side. "We are here to agree to disagree with everyone so far. You all think you know Dr. Burrell, but we," she puts a casual arm across Naydar's shoulders, "We know. We are the ones in that infamous clinic night after night as Ms. Ironsides here runs everyone up and down three corridors." Naydar nods, and points at Maggie.

"She takes no nonsense from anyone. You stay one week you learn, do what she say first time, you don't want her to repeat anything," the shy girl from Benkulu shakes her finger at the group to an enthusiastic response. "Anna is scared of everybody, except Dr. Maggie. Shoot, everybody is scared of Dr. Maggie except her patients. To them she is light, she is peace, she is home."

Anna beams at her younger sister. "Maggie wherever in the world you are, wherever in the world I am, call and I will get there. You are indescribable. Good luck in you new mission, good luck to all you find there. May they love you half as much as we do." The crowd roars.

"Tough act to follow," Sylvie takes the microphone from Anna. "I'm not good at public speaking and I'm very bad at emotional, at least till this month." Here the crowd let's her know they are understanding what she means. "But since it is us, friends here, I will tell you what I know about Maggie Burrell. She is sneaky. Yep, I guess some of you didn't know that, but she had me setting up all sorts of traps for Anna so she would regain her memory. It worked. She is also loud, you should have heard her take that one on," she points toward Rodger who grimaces. "I'm surprised you didn't. She is forgetful, she has forgotten every single thing I said that I ask her not to repeat. She is grumpy when she doesn't get her way," her head shakes, "No, it is true. She is nosy, forget about staying out of her way and keeping your feelings locked up inside you, not going to happen." Anna's mouth has dropped, she cannot believe her Sylvie is talking like this in front of a crowd. She has always been the person in the background. Naydar is giggling and covering her mouth. Michael is nodding his approval. "But believe this, if you are alone and need a friend, this is the one you want. She will be there, she will care as if your problem were her own, she will help if she can and hold you while you cry if she can't. Thank you all for bringing her to me." Sylvie sits to a silent crowd until Dr. Walker starts clapping, then it swells to a crescendo.

Rodger's turn. "What do I say. You all know the Maggie sitting here before you. The Maggie you don't know is the one marching through the heat of Indonesia, headed to who knows what, with some stupid hat on her head and sleeves rolled up to here. You don't know the woman barking out orders to any and all comers. Me, she had washing sheets, washing sheets, yeah, you heard right, and emptying bed pans, and feeding strangers," He shudders at the memory. "Me, the COO of a major international company, was taking notes on the recollections of survivors of a major international incident. But, I am alright with that," this brings lots of giggles from Anna and Naydar, as well as Amur. "I was. After all, this is her department, and as she told me from the beginning, I know nothing about dealing with this sort of event. By the way, she was right about that. However, I am a fast learner. But fast forward, now we are in New York which is my comfort zone, my home. Here I am where I know how to get things done, and then, she does it again. She lets me know when I am out of line, tells me how to manage my business, and puts me in my place letting me know that I would be so sorry if I ever tried to leave her out of the mix about making decisions again." Everyone is pointing at the laughing Maggie and those closest to her are patting her on the back. "Well, Maggie, you were right then too, I am ever so…"

Phil interrupts, "Sorry we are going to have to call this a night, if we are going to get that plane in the air on time." There is a huge groan from the collective company.

Rodger nods, and taking Maggie's hand says, "*Au revoir*, Maggie Burrell till next time."

Maggie blinks back tears as she gets up and walks toward the door, "Thank you my sweet American friends. Come see me sometime, I love you all."

Rodger and Maggie make their way out of the room to the car that is waiting. Phil is already in and has the driver on the way before either is settled. "Are we going to be on time?" Rodger asks.

"Yes, but we won't have any to spare,"

"I wish, I… That was a wonderful send off," she says.

He looks down at her and nods, "It was. When you come back we will have to outdo that for your welcome back party."

Because Phil is urging the driver to push it, they get there with enough time for him to reexaime the flight plan. He boards taking her bag and giving the two a last chance to say goodbye.

She looks at Rodger, "You might want to give that young man a raise."

"I might,"

She holds out her hand, "Well, I guess this is good bye."

He ignores the gesture, taking both of her hands in his own, he raises them to his lips one at a time, tenderly kisses each and says, "No, no way in hell you get rid of me that easy. I'll be in touch, and I will see you every chance I have." He grabs her to him, holds her as if he is holding onto life itself, then he releases her. She walks up the plank into the plane with her head facing backward, her eyes holding on to his face. In she goes, one last wave, and the door shuts. He stands there as the plane moves away from him. He remains there through takeoff and then, when there is nothing else to watch, climbs back into the car and heads to his office. There is still work to be done before the morning. He sighs. Out of the window he sees the planes landing and leaving, and he wonders.

Chapter 43

Back at the office, James greets him with a stiff drink. He gulps down a bit, grimaces, and dives into the work. The team is elbows deep into preparation for tomorrow's hearing. James reads for the legal side, Rodger for the business side and Amur, he is there to help with company security. It is deemed acceptable to have a former undercover operative suggesting possible motives.

The first possibility, is there any likelihood that Anna's identity will be questioned? Amur thinks so, James agrees so they line up and document every ounce of material on her memory loss and return, and all the witnesses that are willing to say that this is the Benson's daughter. They have Michael, Sylvie and Naydar, but it is decided that the wiser course will be to leave the later out of the mix.

Next consideration, is there evidence to confirm Naydar's claim as Carl Benson's daughter. This is tied to Anna's confirmation and the DNA tests which have been corroborated by three different labs, along with Amur's testimony. That is all they have, no papers from Carl, or Maria, nothing from Naydar's mother. DNA will have to suffice.

Rodger brings up the possibility that one or more of the charities that would benefit if Carl's will is broken might put together a push to declare the will null and void. James doesn't think that will be the problem. There is a clause saying if a charity challenges the will, that charity is dropped.

"Do you think there is a chance someone else will claim to be a Benson heir?" Rodger asks.

"Yes, I think with all the speculation surrounding Anna and her memory problems, there is bound to be little Annas emerging from every corner of the globe. I predict we will see at least one from Sweden, and one from the US," Amur replies. "Don't know how they will attempt to prove it, but I bet we will see it."

"Have DNA people ready in the courthouse," is James' suggestion.

"Anything else we need to prepare for?" Rodger looks around, weary heads shake, and the three box up the night's work. Amur and Rodger head to a quiet bar, while James goes home.

It is well after midnight before Rodger is back to the apartment. Memories attack him from every corner. Her smell lingers, he shakes his head as if to rid it of ghosts. Doesn't work. He takes out the cell phone stares at it for a while, then types in a text. "Have a nice flight."

Instantly the reply floods his screen, "Have a nice night, now get to bed, you have a big day tomorrow." Yep, he laughs out loud, shucks the jacket, and prepares for bed, alone.

The morning begins with him awake before the alarm goes off. He struggles to remember why he is too anxious to sleep. Then the bell on his phone sounds and he realizes this is what he is waiting for. The sound that tells him, the CEO of Benson Enterprises, has a jet landing in an airport in Mogadishu, Somalia. He calculates the time it will take to clear customs, load supplies and make the trek to the clinic. His instructions to Phil had been precise, each step to be reported. He glances at the clock, he could try to sleep for another two hours, or he could go work out at the gym and head from there to the court house. He chooses the gym, trying to sleep seems like a waste of time.

He has completed his workout before he rechecks the phone. They have cleared customs and are loading the supplies onto a rented cart. Customs took a while as he had expected. The Somalian Government is tentative about any goods brought in from outside at this time, which is why Phil chose the capital city for entry. Here there would be more personnel to make the process faster. Still, it seems to be taking a long time. Rodger worries, but can do nothing except wait, and depend upon his chosen liaison.

He meets James for breakfast at a small cafe near the court house. Amur will be picking up the girls, and Dave is charged with seeing Dr. Walker, Michael and Sylvie get there on time. The two men discuss the prep from last night going over it in case the night's rest has resulted in any new revelations. None occur. James smiles at his colleague who continues to check his watch, and then phone. It is all he can do to keep from laughing out loud as the fastidious Mr. Madden spills coffee on his sleeve in his haste to retrieve his phone as he hears it beep. The convoy is on the road without interference. Phil's curt text simply says, "You were right ."

When he reads the text aloud, James looks up surprised, "Right about what?" he asks

"They let them pass because they think Phil is in charge. I told him to have Maggie check the boxes with the agents while he talked with the supervisor." The remark draws a sheepish grin from Rodger and a hearty laugh from his companion. And on that relaxed note they depart to the hearing room.

The room is crowded. There are those who should be there, Anna, her doctor, Sylvie, Michael, the staff from the houses who are mentioned in the will, the Benson Enterprise executives directly mentioned in the will including Rodger, James, and Amur. Then there is Naydar, not mentioned by name in the will, along with experts prepared to testify to her necessary inclusion.

The rest of the room is stuffed with media personal, representatives from charities hoping they are mentioned, curious onlookers, and at least five persons hoping to jump into the will on their own status. One is from the legal department of Benson Enterprises, claiming Carl Benson had initiated adoption proceedings before his last trip. Rodger looks at James. He seems quite calm, but, if he knows his companion at all, that young man better hope the court rules in his favor, because he is quite sure, there will be no job at the legal department waiting for him after today.

The court recorder takes down every name of those present, checking it against the list of those who were invited to attend. These people are then sent to another room except for Rodger and James who remain as representatives in the interest of the company. Those wishing to apply for admission into the will are listed on another sheet and sent to a separate waiting area. Naydar is in this group and appears terrified. Rodger smiles, "It will be fine, you are okay." he mouths at her.

One by one, these who are attempting to make their way into the will by whatever pretext are brought in questioned and dismissed. It goes fast, because none of them have any proof to show until we get to the young lawyer. He has a document of adoption that has been filled out. He puts it before the judge who examines it before looking at he young claimant. "Son, you are a lawyer correct?"

The young man nods.

"Then you know," the judge says, "an unsigned document is not admissible as proof, right?"

"It is submitted as proof of intent, Your Honor."

"Un huh," The judge peers over his glasses. "Don't quit your day job. Next."

"But... "

The judge glares at him, sighs, and with a wave of his hand dismisses the claim. "Next"

In walks a shaking Naydar. James rises to speak and Rodger rises to take her arm and lead her to the podium, neither action goes unnoticed.

"Your Honor, I respectfully request that this girl's uncle who has asked to be her legal guardian be present at the questioning. He also has pertinent testimony in her behalf."

The judge looks at the shivering girl, surrounded by the two Benson Company officials. Eyebrows raise, and not all are his. The news contingent is now fully awake and aroused. The judge asks for a name, and Amur is called into the chamber. "Do you represent this girl as a legal council?" asks the judge.

"No sir, I am her relative and have filed to become her guardian until such time as she comes of age." Amur speaks, but it is James that hands over a copy of the papers.

The judge looks at the papers, and then at the assembled group. "Any objections to the man standing in loo of family for uh," he looks down to his list of names, Naydar Parqura?" He reads the name from her passport.

"No," James answers. "We will submit proof that this girl is the natural daughter of Carl Benson and Assandra Parqura, both of whom are now deceased."

"Benson Enterprises is submitting this evidence? Why not change the will, Mr. Stanton, wouldn't that have been easier?"

"Yes sir, it would have, and if the proof had been available one month before it was, I am sure that would have happened. As it is, the will was changed to include all natural children of Carl or Maria Benson. We believe that to be a preemptive change. It is our assertion that this last tragic trip was for the purpose of securing said proof."

"I am thinking there was a challenge for the maternal side also, wasn't there?"

"Yes, but that's been put to rest before today and has been removed from consideration."

"Then this is the only challenge you believe to be valid?"

"Yes, sir. We have DNA samples from Miss Paqura and from Anna Benson that will prove a fraternal sibling connection. We have pictures we can submit of Mr. Benson at a social affair with the challenger's mother, Assandia Parqura. We have experts who will testify to the validity of the DNA samples and, if necessary, we are willing for the court to ask for and secure new tests."

"And is Miss Benson aware and agreeable with these assertions.?"

"Yes, she is. We can call her if you wish to ask further."

"Yes." He nods to the clerk, "Ask Miss Benson to join us."

Anna is brought into the room. She heads to Naydar's side and hugs her. "Everything okay?" she whispers.

The judge clears his throat. "Miss Benson, are you aware of the claims made by this young lady?"

"Yes sir, I am. This is my sister; I have seen the proof."

"And who showed you the proof. Was it the girl's uncle?"

"No sir, it was Mr. Madden."

"And you trust it to be accurate?"

"I did, but the legal team from the company checked it every way they could. I have been swabbed, donated hair, and even my Dad's toothbrush has been tested. I am quite surprised at how thorough the process is."

The room goes silent. Everyone waits as the judge sifts through the submitted paperwork. "Are all these named people on hand to confirm the testing?"

"Yes, Your Honor. They await your pleasure."

"Bring them to my chambers for questioning," he instructs the bailiff. "I'll see them and the two ladies only."

James rises as if to protest but he is waved down. The experts and the girls are escorted out. The waiting begins.

Chapter 44

Every eye is on the clock except Rodger's. He seems engrossed with his phone, glancing at said clock only intermittently. His attention is divided. James watches this curious new side of his colleague. A half hour passes, and the court is called to session again. The judge returns, sits, and promptly dismisses the media from the proceedings, saying "We have agreed to accept the challenge of one person, that of Naydar Paqura. All other challenges are denied. We are now going to proceed to an in depth reading of Carl and Maria Benson's wills. These are private matters and will be conducted as such. If the heirs wish to release copies of the will, that can be done. As of now, this procedure will continue as closed. Escort these people out, and return to the room all those named in the wills." His statement is followed by scraping of chairs and the muttering of disappointed persons including those from news organizations, those from various charities who had hoped to be invited, and from the nosy types who tend to hang around in the hallways of courthouses.

Once the extraneous people are out, the judge resumes, "The will of Maria Benson is straight forward and simple to understand. We will read it first. After the reading, we will pause to allow anyone who chooses to depart the proceedings to do so. We will then begin the reading of Carl Benson's will. Obviously there will be some overlap, but Mr. Benson's will is lengthy, and what we would like to do is to read it in sections. The first pertaining to charitable bequests, the second to individual bequests, and then the meat of the will which concerns his family and outlines his plans for the future of Benson Enterprises. Is that satisfactory to the gathering? Yay, show hands. Nay? The yay's carry. I will now turn this proceeding over to Wallace Miller, lawyer of record for the estate."

Rodger sneaks a peek at James and sees the flush, an outward sign of his feelings.

The named lawyer heads to the front table where he sits, pulls out the paperwork and begins the reading of Maria's will. There are no surprises here, Maria's assets are all liquid and easily assigned. Maria leaves everything to Carl, should he survive her, and to Anna except for a large endowment for Sylvie, a few smaller bequests to the Utley house staff, and a named amount to two of her favorite charities. Sylvie gasps when she hears the amount that she will receive. She will never want for money. Michael is shocked. He spent most of last night telling her that he would look after her as soon as he found a job and secured his work visa. She is glad he didn't know until today how secure she would be.

With Maria's will heard, there is the preordained pause in the proceedings. The staff from the Benson's Utley Estate rise to leave, including Sylvie and Michael. Mr. Miller suggests that she might prefer to remain. She sits. Michael looks at her and pauses, then, when he receives no invitation to stay, he tells her he will wait in the hallway.

Carl's will is the larger and lengthier of the two. It is read by the lawyer also. First are the charitable bequests. This list is longer than Maria's and the amounts are larger. At least two of the groups are breathing a sigh of relief that they didn't proceed with their planned challenge. Then comes those individual bequests, beginning with the bequests to staff at the penthouse. Ellen Hale's intake of breath signals his generosity. The fact that it is in the shape of a trust lets everyone know he hoped these folks would continue to serve his family. The next statement is that he leaves everything to his wife Maria, and any surviving children. Everything takes a while to list: there are a large number of properties, the estate in Utley, the penthouse, and the office building are the physical properties that Carl himself owned. Next are the bank accounts and lock boxes. That listing takes up two pages as there are accounts in various countries where Carl routinely conducted business. After this reading is finished all are dismissed except for the family including Naydar, Sylvie, and those who represent the business.

Carl does not specify a living child, but here today are two making that claim. All the proof that they are the legitimate and legal heirs of Carl Benson is brought forth yet again, examined and accepted. The two girls are declared the daughters and only surviving family of Carl Benson and therefore, his heirs. The inheritance is staggering, and the court acknowledges both the legitimacy of their claims and the need to provide each girl with a legal guardian until the time of their maturity. Carl has not provided suggestions, but here James steps in. He reminds the court that Rodger Madden has filed papers to be named guardian for Anna Benson. He repeats his previous statement that if he has not done so, Amur Saluar will be filing to be named guardian for Naydar.

The judge agrees, "Gentlemen, I would be most willing to agree to the guardianship of the girls funds, but their persons? Is there a second proposal on the table?" Here he turns to stare directly at Sylvie Gilbeck who stares back in confusion.

James looks up, he understands, nods his agreement, and continues, "We believe that the two gentlemen would look after the financial affairs of the young ladies, but that the appointment of Sylvie Gilbeck as their live-in guardian would be a great choice."

Sylvie looks puzzled. Rodger turns to her and explains, "I would look after Anna's financials, but we are asking you to be their substitute mother. We," he points at himself and Amur, "can't do that job, but you have been doing it all this time, unofficially."

The judge folds his hands, "Ms. Gilbeck, are you willing to take on this role in the lives of these two ladies?"

Sylvie looks to first one then the other. Both girls are beaming, eyes pleading. She takes a deep breath, "Do they understand that means they have to mind me?" Everyone breaks into laughter. The deal is done. Sylvie will remain, though not as a nanny, but as an adviser and surrogate mother.

With that part done, only the meticulous business issues remain. The judge asks Anna, Naydar, and Sylvie if they wish to remain. The answer is no. That is what the men have been appointed to do, and the girls are glad that they can escape this part for now.

Mr. Miller picks up the remaining section of the will, that dealing with Benson Enterprises. It is two inches thick and will take some time to go through. He addresses the judge, "At this point, according to the will, I am to retire, and turn my duties over to Mr. Stanton, who is appointed attorney of record for Benson Worldwide Enterprises. He along with two other officers are to go through these papers to put the proposed sections into practice, until such time as they retire, become deceased, or are replaced in their duties by the legal heirs."

James stands, "And who are the two others that will share the directorship of the company?"

"Those two gentlemen there," is the answer. "Mr. Madden is to serve as CEO, and he will appoint and train a new COO, according to the provisions stated herein. Mr. Saluar is to serve as the head of security, and, until there is someone to replace him, as the ambassador to all company properties. It is all spelled out gentlemen and quite frankly, I am delighted to say, it is all yours." With that, he hands the materials to James, shakes hands with Rodger and Amur, nods at the judge and heads for the doorway.

"Well, gentlemen, If you think going through all that will take longer than the fifteen minutes allotted before we break, then I think we should adjourn this hearing until," he looks over at his schedule, "two weeks from today. Will that give you adequate time to discover any problems and suggest fixes?"

"Yes, sir"

"Then this hearing will reconvene at ten A.M. two weeks from this date. See you then, have fun." He rises and leaves the room.

"I don't know about you two, but I'd rather do this in our offices with our people," says Rodger. The others agree. They find the two girls with Sylvie and Michael still chatting in the hallway. Sylvie calls Ellen Hale and the entire group head to the penthouse for a lunch that will be ordered in. It seems to him that eating while discussing the future is becoming a habit, but Rodger does need to talk about what comes next, and everyone would have to eat before the work starts, so back they go to what is now Anna and Naydar's New York home. James goes by and picks up Claire and her ever ready recorder so that everything said can be sorted and put on paper for the court and the Benson company files.

Ellen Hale and staff have the table set and ready. The food is on order as the new faces and voices of Benson Enterprises take their respective places, Sylvie at one end, Rodger at the other. He explains the directive of the court concerning the company and the slate of officers appointed in the will. Anna listens, Naydar is too excited to care, Sylvie focuses on each person's job description. He notices her attention, toasts her with his glass, and waits for the food delivery before going further.

As soon as the meal is finished, Rodger asks Sylvie about her plans. Instead of answering him, she turns and asks Claire and James, "When do you two intend to marry?" The stark question dumbfounds James but amuses Claire.

"Why?"

"I am thinking of my future here. If you marry soon, Claire moves to your place correct?"

"Yes, but how that affects you I don't comprehend." James startled is James at his most pompous.

"I am going to move in here, at least for now," she answers him. "I am thinking of asking Michael to stay in New York. To do that, he needs a place to work and a place to rent. Claire, since we have been living in your apartment, I am hoping you will allow Michael to stay there."

Claire looks at James. "This is not the appropriate time to discuss this. However, I will take it under consideration," her tone is light, but the electricity that passes between the couple is palpable.

Rodger's hooded eyes hide his enjoyment at the obvious discomfort of his staid companion. "That will be something to decide later, I assume?"

James nods, not trusting himself to speak.

"Next, Anna and Naydar, do you trust us to make decisions for you alone, or do you wish to be present?"

Anna thinks, turns to look at Naydar. It appears the two have a non verbal connection, because Anna dips her head before saying, "I think we agree to trust you to make decisions now, as we will both need to learn much more than either of us knows. However, we would like to be kept up to date on what you do. We realize how lucky we are to have you to care for us and the company."

"What else do you need to discuss at this time?" asks Amur. James gives him a relieved glance.

"Education," says Sylvie. "I need help determining what to do about the girls education."

All of the men shake their collective heads. They know less than she does. Ellen Hale walks in at this very moment to ask about dessert. Claire speaks up, "Ms. Hale, do you know anything about education here in the city?"

"Private tutoring?"

Sylvie's face lights up.

"For Naydar I think that will be best," says Amur.

"As for Anna, you might want to have her work with a tutor for a bit to prepare for the application process and to determine what university might best suit her abilities and future plans," adds Claire.

Ms. Hale states she knows someone to call.

It is moving too fast now, and Anna is the one who calls a halt. "We need all this yes, but we also need to catch our breath, slow down, and evaluate."

Rodger stands and at that signal, so do Amur, James and Claire. "You can sort this out together. We have only two weeks to go through everything in Carl's instructions for the future of the company. We need to start today. Girls, expect a report from Ms. Dailey." He pauses, raises his eyebrows, and she says, "Every morning I will send you a report on the previous day's work."

The executives head back to the office to delve into the paperwork while the girls and Michael discuss possible excursions for him while he is in the city. Sylvie and Ellen Hale continue their discussion of the possible opportunities, educational and other, for all three of the youngsters.

Chapter 45

In the offices, Rodger arranges the conference room to hold the men and the files they will require. James takes one side, Amur another. Rodger sets up empty tables in the center to hold all materials they need. His section of the materials will remain on the table to the right of his desk. His desk itself is cleared of any but this day's company work.

The men work in silence, dividing up the sections for instructions according to each man's assignment. They each take notes concerning files to be pulled and employees that will be assigned to help. Claire is overwhelmed. She requests three extra secretaries from the company pool, one to work with each of the executives. She remains the disseminator of information, keeping the flow going as to who needs what and where everyone is in their search.

It is seven before Rodger remembers to check on the other end of the world. They will be asleep there he reasons, but he checks his texts to see if anyone has tried to contact him. There are two messages, one from Phil stating that everyone is in place and Maggie is already working, surprise, surprise. There is also one from the lady in question to tell him to stop worrying, the clinic is up and running, and she is fine. Rodger smiles and replies, "I knew you would have everything running full steam ahead day one. Take care, don't overdo." He starts to set the phone down, knowing she will not see it till the morning.

Shock sets in when there is an immediate answer. "Overdo? Who are you to tell anyone to slow down? I bet you are still at the office." His laughter breaks into the busy room and everyone looks up. He shrugs and they all dive back into the work.

This becomes the norm for the next thirteen days. They assemble in the morning go over what they discovered the day before, ask for suggestions, gather their individual teams and begin again. Each day, Claire sends a progress report to the people both at the penthouse and the courthouse.

At the penthouse, Sylvie is concerned with getting papers for Michael to stay in the country. She enlists Dave's help. He contacts the legal department at Benson Enterprises and they recommend an immigration attorney who confers with both Michael and his mother. The task will go faster if Michael has employment, so he begins a job search.

When Anna uncovers their plan, she sends him to the personnel office at the company, but with the proviso that he understands he will not be an automatic hire but will be interviewed and evaluated like any other applicant. Of course, it doesn't hurt your chances when you are sent by the new owner.

Michael's initial interview is impressive, but the head of personnel services, Thomas Baker, wishes to err on the side of caution, therefore he requests five minutes with the new CEO. CEO Madden is frustrated. He doesn't have five extra minutes in his day because the court date is but two days away, but he takes time to meet in Claire's reception area. He gives the application a cursory glance, frowns at his manager, and asks, "Why are you bringing this to me? Whoever this guy is, he is extremely qualified. Why are we even discussing this?"

"Why did you assume it was a man," mutters Claire, never guessing he will hear, but he does, and rolls his eyes. "Well, I think the young man has some association with Miss Benson, sir. She sent him to us."

Rodger reexamines the folder. "Michael Gilbeck." A short pause is followed by a sigh and, "Yes, give him a temporary position as an intern with the possibility of a permanent position after nine months. Be sure to include an out clause for both parties. What department are you considering for him?"

"We were thinking he might fit into the international exploration and cooperation department.

"Why?"

"He is fluent in three languages and that is indicative of a person proficient at the development of language skills."

"Who do we have heading that right now?"

"That is the problem, as of this moment no one. That was a part of Mr. Saluar's department."

"Okay, let me think and get back to you about a head of department. Meanwhile this will proceed as we discussed. Is that all?" His words are short and his attention has already shifted to the next room.

Thomas Baker takes the file and starts toward the elevator. Rodger says, "Claire, get that into today's notes and remind me in the morning to review the discussion."

Baker almost stops in his tracks, glances back at Claire and Rodger, and totally misses the mark.

Two more fourteen hour days and then it is ready or not. At ten sharp the executives of Benson Enterprises are back with Judge Howser, and the paperwork is submitted for approval. Due to Claire Dailey keeping the court informed on decisions, the entire hearing takes less than two hours. At the conclusion, the directorship of Benson Enterprises is approved, their plan for the future of the company is allowed, and the group as a whole is ready to celebrate. Dave is sent to collect all those at the penthouse. Maggie takes part through via the internet, and everyone is happy, tired, and relieved. Maggie congratulates the entire group before she puts the question out there. "When is the wedding? Where is the honeymoon trip?"

James shrugs his shoulders and points to Claire. "Whenever and wherever she says. She has earned that."

"Here, here," Rodger lifts a glass of Champagne, "and starting immediately after this celebration, everyone involved will take three days off, including all this office's staff, executives, and any other involved company employees. You also Dave."

"And me boss," asks Phil?

"You might have to put your time off back a bit. I have one more task for you before your week off."

Phil flashes the rakish grin, "I thought you might."

The celebration breaks up a few hours later, and everyone heads to freedom. James and Claire to finalize wedding plans, Amur to check out his new offices, the penthouse occupants to a broadway play, and Rodger to the airport with Phil. Next stop Somalia and a brief two day reunion with Maggie. Once there, he is reduced to all the jobs he remembered from Benkulu, including listening to victims, recording their stories, and analyzing data.

By Monday afternoon he is back in the office. Tuesday James reports back to work sporting the biggest smile anyone has ever seen on him. He and Claire were wed at the courthouse on Monday and are busy planning a well deserved honeymoon. He is happy to be in the office today because the last two days were hectic. They have moved Claire out of the apartment and into James' place. Michael is to assume the position as subtenant of said apartment.

The girls head to Utley for a while to recoup, start their studies, and explore their new relationship. Their new tutor, Justin Allen, is busily working up each girl's curriculum. The world, this world, returns to something resembling normal.

Epilogue

It has been two years and two days since the largest recorded tsunami in history sent his cozy world into bedlam. Rodger Madden is headed out to the site of yet another disaster. And Maggie. He will be there for a three week stay at the latest Doctor's International Clinic to host the Burrell team from Australia. There have been visits with Maggie twice in Somalia, twice in New York, and once in Australia in these two years. This time it will be Haiti. He wonders if she knows about his new connection with Doctor's International.

Dave's assistant comes back to the cabin to announce their imminent arrival into Port-au-Prince. Rodger remembers two years back to his landing in Darwin, and wonders if Dave has a "friend" who will meet him on the tarmac as Phil did. He also wonders if Phil's many "friends" are aware of his marriage or the impending baby girl who will keep him anchored to his desk as head of Benson's logistics unit for the foreseeable future.

The plane touches down and taxis to a stop. There is someone waiting on the tarmac for him, but she is not a "friend" of Dave's and not a patient lady.

"It's about time you got here," Maggie starts before planting a light kiss on his cheek. "We are full and overflowing, and I don't have time to loll around waiting on the volunteer help."

"I love you, too," he answers as he gathers her in for a much longer embrace. "And I am your boss for the next three weeks. At least I am the clinic's boss. Doctor's International sent me to analyze and recommend regulations to streamline procedures for setting up and running emergency response units like yours." He eyes her, waiting for the response. It isn't what he expected.

"You know, that is a good idea. You are great at figuring out what is missing, what is needed, and setting up channels for the distribution of resources wherever they are most valuable. Excellent idea. Whose was it?"

Now that's the Maggie he knows. "Mine. It is win, win. This means our company, Benson Enterprises, will receive all sorts of great press for humanitarian works. Anna and Naydar will be asked to pull in the society of New York, which will involve them in New York society. It will make our staff feel important and worthy, and I will get to spend time each year with my favorite doctor. How's that for inspiration?"

Maggie laughs, grabs his hand as they saunter to her jeep. "Hop in, boss." She smiles, "It just might be a bumpy ride."

"Somehow, I would not be surprised."

More books by Janie Hopwood
from Aakenbaaken & Kent

The Forever Child

Gene, a most enterprising young man, flees security toward the unknown — dependent only upon his own ingenuity. He lands in the middle of the red-light district of Albany, Georgia and becomes an integral part of Madame Valdimer's household. Meanwhile, Sarah, snatched from this very house only a short time before, is separated from family, handed into servitude, used, and abused. Fate helps her to escape and she rushes back to the house where she meets Gene. Amid the backdrop of a great depression, in a changing nation that moves rapidly from horse power to "horsepower," to air power, and war, two children, lost to those they were born to, torn from those they lived with, find refuge in a most ludicrous place where they create family. A struggle to survive becomes a struggle to succeed supported by the most unlikely cast.

Beck House
(forthcoming)

Beck House continues the story of Rena Beck, a twice-widowed woman who provides for her six daughters by transforming their home into a boarding house where guests are fed sumptuously and roomers are treated like family. Rena is a mother hen who protects her daughters without smothering them, an entrepreneur who takes advantage of every opportunity that comes her way, and a sympathetic, caring, landlady who takes on the woes of the world through her colorful boarders. She faces the fight of her life when Sumter County tries to take her house and land by eminent domain. Rena has always treated others justly and cannot believe that someone would treat her otherwise. How she faces this final battle is characteristic of her life's story, a story you do not want to miss.

Other books from Aakenbaaken & Kent

A Summer to Remember
by
Amy M. Bennett

 Bonney Police detective J.D. is trying to focus on his budding relationship with Corrie Black, owner of the Black Horse Campground. But when a serial killer case he thought he solved is reopened, he fears killer is poised to strike again. Who held a grudge against the three cold-case victims? And who is the next target? With the help of Bonney County Sheriff Rick Sutton, J.D. probes the memories of several Bonney residents who knew the victims and begins to make connections. Then another death occurs. Corrie is attacked and loses her memory, including the identity of her attacker. Will she remember what happened? Or will she end up as a memory?

Rough & Polished
by
t. lewis

 What if you made choices in your life that haunted you forever? What if you didn't? Raegan Phillips Bernardini did both. Someone once told her that if she hadn't made mistakes in her life then she hadn't lived much. Based on that theory, Rae had lived as much as she wanted. From Africa to Atlanta, Rae had left a trail of casualties in her wake. Not intentionally of course. She was a child; mistakes would be made. Watching her father had taught her the ins and outs of illegal diamond trading, and her innocence had been the casualty. In Atlanta, wild and unmanaged, she followed in his footsteps. Stealing the diamonds from her wealthy clients had come easy. A dangerous lover had made it possible. The people she'd trusted had burned her; life had burned her. So Rae moved on day in and day out, wearing her scars and causing them for others. Then there was Daniel.

In God's Trailer Park
by
Susan Lang

In God's Trailer Park is an unforgettable novel that, with tenderness and humor, depicts the nitty-gritty lives of residents of a small Mojave Desert town. The story is bursting with indelible characters: Social worker Charlotte Sall does her best to plug up holes in the dam holding back the flood of miseries threatening to inundate her clients' lives–all the while dealing with issues that arise with her own children. Recently widowed with a seven-day-old baby, Linda Farley, stubbornly persists in finding work, determined not to let a flood of bad fortune drown her and her young children. Waitress Alice Landers tries her best to protect her schizophrenic son from himself. All of these and other quietly heroic characters find themselves entangled in the mysterious disappearance of a newborn belonging to one of the residents. The diverse ways the characters face down their hardscrabble lives gives a vision of hope to us all.

Roadkill Arts and Other stories
by
Niles Reddick

You never know who's going to turn up in one of Niles Reddick's stories…a lapsed evangelist working as a motel night clerk, a bargain-hunting father, an aunt who makes peroxide tea, or a seventeen-year-old girl just admitted to a mental hospital…not to mention wild dogs, snakes, and UFOs! Each one of these short, down-to-earth and often surprising stories packs a considerable punch. Reddick's characteristic humor allows for some revelations as well." — Lee Smith, North Carolina author of *Family Linen, Fair and Tender Ladies, Saving Grace, The Last Girls, On Agate Hill,* and *Dimestore, a Writer's Life.*

See our complete list of titles at:
Aakenbaakenandkent.com

Although all Aakenbaaken & Kent books are available online from all booksellers, we recommend you buy or order them from your local independent bookstore. If you do not have an indie bookstore, you can order them from Book & Table, an independent bookstore in Valdosta, Georgia where all Aakenbaaken & Kent books are discounted 10% and shipping is free. Ordering is easy. Just email the store at:

bookandtablevaldosta@gmail.com.

CPSIA information can be obtained
at www.ICGtesting.com
Printed in the USA
FFHW021654291018
49004140-53258FF

9 781938 436437